ALSO BY JIM HAYHURST, SR.

THE RIGHT MOUNTAIN

Lessons From Everest
On the Real Meaning of Success

In 1988, Jim Hayhurst, a forty-seven year old ex-advertising executive, became the oldest member of the Canadian Expedition to Mount Everest.

The Right Mountain is the riveting story of that climb. He tells you about the life-threatening experiences that affected each member of the team. He describes the critical choices that had to be made, and the lessons that were learned as a result. But it is much more than an adventure story. It is about defining success for yourself—on your own terms—in your personal life or in your career.

The Right Mountain is inspirational. The story is dramatic. The metaphors compelling. And the messages it contains will stay with you long after the story is over.

Praise for
THE RIGHT MOUNTAIN

"I was having a rather dreary, non-motivated, end-of-summer, no-holidays-planned, should-I-change-my-job sort of day. Browsing through a local bookshop, I picked up *The Right Mountain* and spent the evening reading it. Thank you. What a lovely inspirational story!"
> —Jennifer Neal
> London, England

"There is no better motivational message about team building, knowing yourself, and defining success for your life than *The Right Mountain*. Jim's message empowers your people to accomplish their business and personal goals."
> —Thomas P. Seay
> Executive Vice-President
> Wal-Mart Stores, Inc.

"Your book, right from the preface, put my life and goals into perspective. I would like to thank you for placing your feelings, goals, and successes in words. This way people like myself can learn to realize what their 'Core Values' are in life."
> —Sue Edmiston
> Port Perry, Ontario

"It might be a little exaggerated to state that you changed my life, but reading *The Right Mountain* put so many things in perspective for me. I daresay, you have helped me become a better human being!"
> —Eva Lykkegaard
> Denmark

"Experiential education at its best! Jim's story pushes us to extend ourselves, to grow, to dream. And he points out the difference between our dreams for ourselves and those others have for us. A valuable lesson."
> —Wendy Pieh
> Former Program and Executive Director
> Outward Bound

"One morning I walked into a bookshop and your book was 'looking at me.' I skimmed through it, was captured by the photographs, layout and subject. Six hours after buying it, I had finished the book—it would have been great to read another 178 pages!"
> —Simone Oortman
> New Zealand

"It is impossible to read *The Right Mountain* without reflecting on your own life. I enjoyed this book immensely."
> —Dr. Leonard Berry
> Marketing Professor, Texas A&M University,
> and Author of *On Great Service*

"Great story...great message! There are lessons here for everyone in the family and many at work. I want them all to read it. It's the kind of book I like to keep on my bedside table for regular referral. It will help me squeeze that little bit more out of life."
>
> —John M. Thompson
> Senior Vice-President and Group Executive
> IBM

"A marvellous guide to our own inner journeys…with an insightful way of measuring success."
>
> —Reverend Chris Lehman
> United Church of Canada

"I took *The Right Mountain* home and read it cover to cover the following afternoon. The book was easy to read, which made it that much harder to put down. Thank you for recharging my batteries and reminding me of some of the basics that we all forget too quickly."
>
> —Dick Smeelen
> Toronto, Ontario

"*The Right Mountain* is a masterpiece. Thank you for writing such a fine book."
>
> —Salman Mir
> Pakistan

"I have just finished reading *The Right Mountain* and had to write and thank you for writing such a great book. I am a mountaineering book collector, bookseller, and climber and have read just about every book written on Everest. Yours is so refreshing, so unlike all of the others, and so thought-provoking that I will be asking my climbing teammates to read it."
>
> —Greg Glade
> Top of the World Mountaineering & Polar Books
> Williston, Vermont

"Your book is an incredible inspiration to me."
　　　—Diane Chesla
　　　　Milton, Ontario

"*The Right Mountain* is a compelling and inspirational book."
　　　—Peter Williams
　　　　President
　　　　Equitable Life of Canada

"*The Right Mountain* is terrific! It is such a thought-provoking and gripping read that I simply couldn't put it down! I am certain that I will refer to it and ponder its pearls of wisdom many more times."
　　　—A. Parasuraman
　　　　Professor and Holder of the James McLamore Chair in
　　　　Marketing, University of Miami
　　　　Miami, Florida

"Last night I sat down and read your book and did not get up until I'd finished it. I was completely captivated....Thanks for sharing your story."
　　　—Mary Hanley Rodney
　　　　London, Ontario

"Thank you for writing the book, telling your story about Everest. *The Right Mountain* was both inspirational and educational, but beyond that a beautiful publication, it is simply a delight to own."
　　　—Robert McLean
　　　　Shepparton, Australia

Where Have I Gone Right?

Where Have I Gone Right?

The Right Mountain Guide
to Getting the Job and
Life You Want

JIM HAYHURST, SR.

John Wiley & Sons Canada, Ltd.

National Library of Canada Cataloguing in Publication

Hayhurst, Jim
    Where have I gone right? : the Right Mountain guide to getting the job and life you want / Jim Hayhurst.

Includes index.
ISBN 0-470-83354-8

    1. Success. I. Title.

HF5549.5.C35H39 2004   650.1   C2003-906703-3

Production Credits
Cover & interior text design: Interrobang Graphic Design Inc.
Page 95: *The Wagon Master* by David Sanders
Printer: Tri-Graphic Printing Ltd.
Printed in Canada
10 9 8 7 6 5 4 3 2 1

John Wiley & Sons Canada, Ltd
22 Worcester Road
Etobicoke, Ontario
M9W 1L1

My mother, Jean, longed to write a book, but never did.
Her spirit is a part of my writing.

CONTENTS

Acknowledgements

When I left the advertising business, I had no idea what I was going to do with the rest of my working life. Outward Bound Canada was my bridge, and I want to thank Ian Yolles for his listening skills as I wandered across that bridge.

Eric Barton introduced me to outplacement counseling, and gave me the opportunity to see my skills in that area. Dr. Tiiu Slankis intimidated me, and then became a mentor, friend, and associate as we helped others.

Gay Marshall was my assistant at Hayhurst Advertising and guided me as we set up The Career Centre. Her insights into clients, and her willingness to challenge me, made us a formidable team in our early years of counseling.

Chris Lehman has been a business partner of mine for over 22 years. His intellectual curiosity, and our resulting discussions, have contributed mightily to my understanding of jobs, careers, and life. This book, and any ensuing Guides, are the result of his strategic business insights. Thanks Chris.

Ian Cameron, Jane Sorenson, and Michael Reddy went through our program at various stages, and then became counselors with us, adding their unique perspectives to the process.

Karen Herder and Maggie Malewski went through our program in 2002/2003, and reviewed this manuscript. They each added valuable insights, and pointed out gaps and inconsistencies between the one-on-one version of the program and this book. These contributions have definitely made it a better book.

My daughter Barb—you first met her as Boo in *The Right Mountain*—is Vice President, Operations at Verity International Limited, an outplacement firm. She continually challenges my assumptions, and adds to my understanding of people and the process.

Jimmy, my son, was at Everest with me, or perhaps I was with him. Much of my ability to recognize and give credit to good ideas from others comes from his constant searching for ideas and then prodding me to consider them. He has been the marketing director for this book, and deserves credit for the success it might be.

When I was writing this section, my first thought to describe Cindy, my eldest daughter, was that she was my hero. At first I wondered where that thought came from, and then I realized that she was the first in our family to pursue professional writing as a vocation, but put it on hold to be a wife to Scott, and a mother and coach to Ben, Cameron, and Griffin. That truly is making a difference.

Paddy, Boo's husband, reviewed and gave me ideas for this book. He has a way of describing everyday situations in such a *sartre* way that he brings smiles to all our faces.

Beth, Jimmy's wife and mother of Statten, Quinn, and Tatum, manages her father-in-law and her husband's partner, both of whom are me, with dexterity and love. Thanks Wink.

Scott, Cindy's husband, lives daily by his Core Values, respect for others, and integrity. I treasure his friendship.

Liz Grogan, my fair lady, patiently pestered me with ideas. I know I don't seem to always be listening, but I am. I'm just a little slow. You make me better, in lots of ways.

My friend Chris Dobson, Dobbie, went back to college in his sixties to take philosophy courses. He pushes my thinking always, and when we talk about this book and its core philosophy, he reminds me that Aristotle long ago said that happiness occurs when the soul is acting in accordance with virtue and virtue is the disposition to do the *right* (thing). So I guess this book is built on a long ago discussed premise.

Thank you Karen Milner, Executive Editor at Wiley Canada, for your confidence, insights, patience, and sense of humor. I told you I love you, and then told you I hate you, at the various stages of the writing of this book. Both are true, but I know you are a true friend and supporter.

Michelle Bullard, my editor, quickly understood what I was trying to say and do with this book, and helped me both organize and articulate it much, much better. Thanks Michelle.

We had a devil of a time finding a title for this book. Finally I turned to a pro, John Burghardt, who has been on the creative side of the keyboard for longer than either of us will admit. He phoned three days later: "I've got it." And he did. Thank you John.

Both Brian Harrod and Richard Ponsonby, a pair of graphic artists extraordinaire, took us through cover concepts and inspired this arresting book cover. Thank you. Christine Rae gave her all to make the cover powerful. Thanks, Christine.

And to the hundreds of individuals that have gone through The Right Mountain Career Program, thanks. You all taught me something that improved the process. And you also taught me that none of us is better than the other; we are all just different.

Mihn and debi labored to read my scrawl. I handwrote this manuscript, and they, often under huge time pressures from me, brought it to fruition. Thank you for your patience and skill.

This manuscript was written in Algonquin Park, Canada, and overlooking the beach in Naples, Florida. Thank you to my family for the peace and quiet in "The Park," and thanks to our neighbors in Naples, Patty and Marshall, for the use of their villa when I needed to get out of our place.

As in the original book, *The Right Mountain*, most of the photos are by Jim Jr., a few by me, two are from Jim Elzinga of Everest Light, and one from Barry Blanchard, our leader. They help, I believe, crystallize issues and metaphors.

Most of the shadows in our life
are caused by standing in our own sunshine.
—unknown

Introduction

You can improve your ability to make virtually any significant decision in your life by first asking yourself this question: **WHO AM I?**

Getting a job.

Changing your career.

Returning to the workforce.

Facing early retirement.

Trying to find balance.

Searching for job satisfaction.

WHO AM I? is a summary of your Core *Skills* (functional, personality, and knowledge), your Core *Interest* areas (people, data, or things), and your Core *Values*.

When you know these cores, and very few of us genuinely do, and have found a distinct way to articulate them, which this book helps you find. Then you can use them as a template to test job, career, organization and life decisions to see if there is a match.

And if there is a match, then you will be happy and satisfied.

And if you are satisfied, you will be motivated.

And if you are motivated, you will be successful.

So, it all starts with **WHO AM I?**

If you don't know and can't articulate, in a unique way, the answer to that question, then this book, this process, is for you.

It may reassure you to know that you are not alone in this lack of understanding of who you are.

I have asked this question of company presidents, professors, students, top civil servants, graduates of outplacement programs, four of the top insurance salesmen in the world, and dozens of others, and each and every one of them has, after describing themselves, stopped and said something like:

"That wasn't very good, was it?"

"I sound like everybody else."

"Gee, that's tough, that's hard to do."

"Wow! And I thought I knew myself. But when you put it that way…."

"I described my job. But that's not who I am…is it?"

"No one has ever asked me that before."

Yet you have to understand *who you are* before you can decide what you are going to do to ensure you are fulfilled at work, at home, and at play. And so you can feel confident making difficult life decisions and having positive, healthy relationships.

On a micro level, if you are starting a job search, you have to know who you are because each and every job interview starts out with basically the same question: "Well, tell me about yourself! Who are you?" And it doesn't matter how old you are—22, 33, 44, 55, or more—the question is still the same: *Who are you?* And, you have three minutes, just three minutes, to make an impression and arouse curiosity in the listener.

Why just three minutes? Because 90% of the impression you make happens within the first three minutes. Think about it. Think of the people you've met recently. Think of cars, of music. Think of paintings. You form an opinion quickly, usually in less than three minutes.

Are the things you see and hear unique, do they appeal to you, or is it just more of the same?

In an interview situation, you obviously need to stand out from the crowd, so you need to find a unique description of yourself to make a lasting and favorable impression.

An interviewer in a job search has dozens of interviews, usually one after another, and has probably done hundreds in the last year. So, in order to stand out, you have to say something unique. And you have to do it quickly because, after three minutes, she is either bored or intrigued. Those are the only options.

If your answer to "Who are you?" is a lot of generic words and phrases:

"I like people."

"I'm good with computers."

"I'm family oriented."

"I'm passionate."

"I'm very creative. I write a lot."

…then you sound like everyone else who has been interviewed. To increase your chances of getting invited back for a second and third interview, you have to first find out who you really are, and then find a way to dramatically and effectively introduce yourself.

And, much more importantly, *you'll* then know who you are. And that means you'll have both the ability to decide what you want to do, and the confidence to do it, professionally and personally. You'll be able to make the best career and life decisions.

When things are difficult, when bad things happen, we tend to ask ourselves, "Where have I gone wrong?" This is exactly the wrong question to ask. The right question, the question that opens doors, creates opportunities, and helps take you where you want to go is, *"Where have I gone right?"*

And this book helps you answer that question. It takes lessons from my best-selling book, *The Right Mountain: Lessons from Everest on the Real Meaning of Success,* and combines it with the process of The Right Mountain Career Centre, to provide you with a workbook, to help you discover and articulate who you are. And then it helps you figure out what you want to do with your life.

Where did the phrase "The Right Mountain" come from? Here's the story.

The Right Mountain

In 1988, I was running our Career Centre, which offers a program based on the principle that you have to know who you are before you can decide what you want to do. The thesis of the program is that you look for a match between *who you are* (**your Core Skills**, **Interests**, and **Values**), and a job, career, an organization or components of your life. And when you find a match, you'll love the job, thrive in the life, and have no regrets.

That same year, my son Jimmy and I were part of a Mount Everest expedition. I've included some photos in this book to help demonstrate some of the issues facing us on the mountain are metaphors for issues in our day-to-day lives.

During the climb, two men on the French Team climbing beside us died. Pierre died because his *Core Skills* did not match the needs of the mountain. Everest was not *The Right Mountain* for him. Michel died because his *Core Values* did not match the needs of the mountain. Everest was not *The Right Mountain* for him.

Let me explain.

Jim Jr. and Jim Sr. at Base Camp, north side of Everest, 1988.

As Pierre climbed higher and higher, his body did not acclimatize to the continually reducing air pressure. The inside of his head began to expand, a problem called cerebral edema. Eventually, because his system was not able to control this expansion, the inside of his head imploded down his spinal cord, and he died a vicious, writhing death.

Pierre should have stopped, turned around, and climbed back down to lower altitudes where the air pressure was greater and the swelling would stop. But he didn't. He pressed on, continuing to climb, continuing to feel the increasing pain of the headaches caused by the expansion. He continued on because he believed that mountain climbing was a tough sport, that there should be lots of pain, and that the victors climbed through the pain. He knew he was tough, resilient, and persistent, and he wanted desperately to get to the top.

But if he had compared these skills (tough, resilient, persistent—yes, these are skills) with the needs of the mountain to see if there was a match, he would have realized that, while Everest demands these skills, it also demands skills such as patience and sensitivity to warning signs (headaches). His skills, therefore, did not match the needs of the mountain.

He should have either modified his behavior (been more patient, more sensitive, and not just climbed through the pain), or stayed off the mountain.

He didn't, and it cost him his life.

He was not on *The Right Mountain*…for his Core Skills.

Michel's Core Value was independence, and so when the climbing leader said the team was going to turn back 200 vertical yards from the peak, Michel said no, he was going to go on. All his life he had wanted to climb Everest, and he wasn't going to turn back now.

True to his Core Value of independence, he continued to climb, alone, up into temperatures of 60 degrees below zero,

into winds of over 150 miles per hour, and into altitudes where over two feet of snow could fall in an hour and it could snow for six hours.

After these deaths, we did a lot of thinking, a lot of introspection. What were *our* individual skills? Were they a match for Everest?

You can't climb alone in these conditions.

Michel couldn't. And he died, alone.

If he had tried to match his Core Value of independence with the needs of Everest, he would have realized there was no match. And he would have either modified his behavior (and climbed down with the team), or stayed off the mountain.

He didn't, and it cost him his life.

Everest was not *The Right Mountain* for his Core Values.

The French team, 200 vertical yards from the peak, 28,428 feet up Mount Everest.

At The Right Mountain Career Centre, we believe it is just as important here at home, in our jobs, in our relationships, and as we develop our lives, to know our Core Skills and our Core Values, so we can choose *The Right Mountain* for us.

And while we won't necessarily die if we don't know who we are, we may find ourselves in jobs, relationships, or lives that are not a match for us.

And if there is no match, we will not be satisfied.

And if we are not satisfied, we will not be motivated.

And if we are not motivated, we will not be successful.

And, if we are not successful, we will, metaphorically, die.

And so *The Right Mountain* presentations to organizations around the world, that grew out of this climb, and my first book, *The Right Mountain*, were designed inspire people to stop and think about who they are, and test that against what they want to do with their lives, before they make vital decisions.

The Right Mountain Career Centre Program and our workshops are designed to help individuals work through a unique process to figure out who they are, and then to find a match with jobs, careers, organizations, lives, and relationships.

This book, **Where Have I Gone Right?**, is for those people who can't come to Toronto to do the program. It is a guidebook based on our proven processes to help individuals, step by step, figure out who they are, so they can make the best career and life decisions.

Developing the Process

I was 45 years old and out of a job.
I thought my situation was unique.
But so do you.
So does everyone.

The uniqueness of my situation was due to the fact that I had sold a business and had some money—not enough to live like a king, but some money. However, I knew I wanted, and needed psychologically, to work.

I had a no-compete clause that formed part of the sale agreement of my business. The purchaser wanted this because they didn't want me to take the money for the business and then just walk across the street, start up again, and steal back my former clients. And I accepted it because I thought that after 22 years in the industry, I was ready for a change. The downside of the no-compete clause was that I couldn't do any of the things that I had spent my whole working career doing: advertising, marketing, public relations, research.

So, what was I going to do? What kind of job would suit me? And how would I get that job?

Like many of us, I thought the job would come looking for me. It didn't. I thought people, my friends, my peers would phone me with suggestions. They didn't. I thought I had a high enough profile in the business community that there might be a bidding war for my services. There wasn't. I was out of the loop.

I rented a small office, eventually figured out how to get a phone installed—how do you get a phone when you don't have a phone? It never rang. I fell deeper and deeper into that dark hole called *maybe I'm no good, maybe I'll never find a job*. My confidence disappeared.

I was in that dark hole for almost a year. And then I finally hit bottom. I realized that nobody could help me but me. I had to look up, not down.

I realized that instead of looking at the bad things that were happening, had happened, most of which were only in my mind, I should look at the good things.

I should look at *where I had gone right*.

At first I was totally overwhelmed by the challenge. The only way to tackle it, I realized, was to break it down into bite-sized pieces.

One of the first things that came up when I looked at *where have I gone right?* was my experience with Outward Bound. So I got back in touch with them and got re-involved as a volunteer.

But what about a job? Well, I realized that I had gone right in my careers in marketing and advertising. And our success, my success, had always come when we had first talked to and listened to our customers and learned about them and their needs.

So I decided to talk to, and listen to, people that felt good about their jobs, their careers, and their lives. Why them? Because I wanted to find a job, a career, a life that I would feel good about. And I wanted to learn how they had made their choices.

LESSONS FROM EVEREST
Bite-Sized Pieces

Early in the acclimatization trek for Everest, I realized we were facing a 120-mile walk and climb...before we even got to Everest. I was overwhelmed. I didn't think I could do it. Finally I realized that if I wanted to do it, and I had come too far to turn back now, I needed to break this 120 miles down into bite-sized pieces and take them on one at a time. So I set incremental goals of turns in the path, the next hilltop, huts, and, when I reached each goal, I set another. Then another. I took on the hike, and then the mountain, in bite-sized pieces. We should take on life's challenges in bite-sized pieces.

I went in search of people who loved what they did and felt successful. And I listened to what they had to say.

I listened to corporate executives, civil servants, firefighters, people in not-for-profit organizations, doctors, teachers, lawyers, marina operators, mechanics, ranchers, and lots of "regular" people who loved their lives. I listened to over 100 women and men.

And I reviewed their comments, looking for patterns.
The patterns popped out:

"I'm successful because I'm motivated. I'm motivated because I feel satisfied."

There it is! In my terms, the keys to success:

Satisfaction ⟶ Motivation ⟶ Success

I'm sure I wasn't the first one to discover this, but I'd learned it my way, experientially, by doing rather than reading about it, and so I truly understood and believed it.

But what could I do with this insight? I wasn't sure, so I parked it and went searching for another mountain to climb, metaphorically.

I decided I needed to know more about how people got hired. What were interviewers looking for?

I called some peers from my previous business life and asked for introductions to their human resources people. And I started interviewing again.

I listened to people who did the hiring in big business, small business, governments, and the not-for-profits. I branched out and talked to people who owned antique stores, restaurants, service stations, and small manufacturing businesses. I listened, again, to over 100 women and men.

And then I distilled what they had said. It turned out to be consistent and fairly simple. Hirers wanted potential employees to help them make the hiring decision easy, by telling them:

1. Who they are—their skills, their interests, and their values

2. What they had done—where they have gone right—their accomplishments

3. How these accomplishments were relevant to the job being discussed

And, interestingly enough, when I asked those who just plain loved their lives, the same elements of success appeared: they used their Core Skills in areas that matched their interests and in environments that corresponded with their values. It was consistent.

It seemed simple in concept but apparently it was deceptively difficult in execution. Virtually all hirers said very few applicants could answer these three questions and from my research, I knew far too many people were unhappy with their lives.

I thought about it.

Who am I? What are my skills, interests, and values? Nobody had ever asked me that question before. Indeed, *who am I*?

What have I accomplished? Most of us don't think we've accomplished very much and, if we have recently been fired, our confidence is at a very low ebb. *What have I accomplished*?

How is it relevant? Well, this is particularly difficult if you are wanting to make a career change. Are any of your old experiences and accomplishments relevant or transferable?

It seems I had completed my research, gotten to the top of these particular peaks. What do I do now? What is the next step?

I decided to see if these two insights were connected in any way. And they were.

Employers want to know:

Who you are, where you've gone right, what you've accomplished.

Applicants could look at:

What they'd accomplished (where they had gone right) to figure out who they are.

And in a job interview situation, both parties could see if there was any relevance to the job being discussed. A win, win.

I designed a process to help individuals, including myself, to uncover my accomplishments. *Where I have gone right*. And that process became our Career Centre, and now this book. The essence of the process is that you:

1. Look where you've gone right, what you've accomplished, particularly events that gave you a real sense of satisfaction.

2. Tease these accomplishments apart to find the *skills* you have used, the *interest areas* involved, and the *values* inherent in the activities.

The theory, as mentioned earlier, is that you then match up those skills, interests, and values with jobs, careers, and organizations, and, for those not looking for work, with life decisions. And when there is a match, you can be sure that you will be:

• Satisfied

• Therefore motivated

• Therefore successful, in both an organization's terms and your own terms

The perfect circle!

To test this theory, I wrote a self-assessment guidebook. I checked it out with some psychologists to see if it could be harmful. They said no. I then took myself through the process.

The result? I discovered *who I really am*.

And, once I discovered this truth, it helped me understand why I had actually done well in some jobs. And why I hadn't done so well in other jobs. And why some life decisions and relationships appealed to me more than others.

The revelation was incredible. The outcome was a real release.

These insights gave me the confidence to start what became The Right Mountain Career Centre, and to develop the tools to help others go through the program so they too could achieve their dreams.

And that's why I wrote this book, to help individuals like you discover *who are you*, so you can find a job, a career, an organization, and a life that you love and one in which you thrive.

As I think about this process and the title *Where Have I Gone Right?*, I remember that when I felt overwhelmed on Everest, one of my climbing partners, Dixon, had tried to convince me to look back at the things I had done right—the cliffs I had already climbed—in order to get the confidence to take on the upcoming challenges. He tried to get me to do what this book will help you do.

LESSONS FROM EVEREST
You Can Learn a Lot by Looking Back

At a point in time on the acclimatization climb, we had a particularly daunting cliff in front of us. I saw Dixon, one of our climbers, looking back.

I pointed to the cliff in front of us and suggested he might more usefully look at the challenges facing us. He should visualize the upcoming challenges, goal set, imagine himself climbing.

He nodded but suggested that I look back at the cliff we had just climbed and remember my trepidation as we stood at the bottom of it. It was too big, too tough. But then we had climbed it. He suggested that if I looked back at that accomplishment I might develop the confidence to take on the challenge, the cliff in front of us.

I did. It worked. And it works in other contexts too.

The Right Process
How to Use This Book

The process is, as all good processes are, really very simple. Here are the steps this book will take you through.

Part One: Who Am I?

1. First we ask you to make a list of *accomplishments.*

   Go back through your life, education, work experience, volunteer activities, extra-curricular activities, and personal times, and find events where you have gone right. These are accomplishments. They are not necessarily big, earth-shaking events. And they are not necessarily accomplishments that received praise from your parents, teachers, peers, or society. But they are events that gave *you* satisfaction.

2. Then we ask you to break the accomplishments down into four components.

   I)   First you will look for your *skills.*

You will tease these accomplishments apart, to pull out the skills you used in each of these events.

II)   Then you will look for your *interest areas*.

You will learn that there are only three interest areas in life—people, data, and things—and you will discover their priority for you.

III)   Next you will look at *values*.

You will find the values that are common in each of these accomplishments. Values are the most underrated, under-utilized, and misunderstood element of our being. And they are, without doubt, the most important. This section will specifically prioritize your values.

IV)   Finally you will look at *relationships*.

While this is not a selling point while searching for a job, it is important in selecting an organization and in the other parts of your life. Your satisfaction and your success are greatly affected by your relationships with others. This section helps you identify the characteristics of people you relate best with and to, in both job and general life situations.

3.   Next you will dig deep to find your *Core Accomplishments*.

This is a review section, and if necessary, a revision section. Earlier, you listed your accomplishments, then teased out your skills, interests, values, and relationships. Now you will review your accomplishments to see if they each truly demonstrate these core elements. Perhaps you will discard some, or even rewrite some to better demonstrate the real accomplishment. In some cases, this review will reveal other, often more relevant, accomplishments.

4. Finally you will narrow down these Core Accomplishments, these examples of *where you have gone right*, into vivid demonstrations of *who you are*. You do this by:

I)   First finding a *Reference Point*.

This Reference Point is the key to your very being. It is an event, or a moment, that found you feeling good/fulfilled/satisfied, being yourself—one that you can forever compare other activities with. It is a template that quickly, and graphically, illustrates your skills, interests, values, and relationships. This Reference Point will enable you to positively decide whether you are on The Right Mountain with any job, career, or life decision that you are making.

II) Next by seeing if you can find a *Personal Allegory*.

This is a unique and very memorable way of describing your Reference Point. An allegory is a story, a picture, a thing in which the meaning or message—who you are—is presented symbolically. Not all of us think allegorically; only about 40% of our Career Centre clients do. If you do, it is a fun, unique, and memorable way of describing yourself.

Part Two: Getting the Job and Life You Want

In this part, we will walk you through the Job Search process:

1. Understanding the Hiring Process.

2. Creating Your Résumé.

3. Networking.

4. Informational Interviewing.

5. The Interview and the Job Offer.

Then we will discuss how *who am I?* is used when looking at Balance and Life decisions.

Now you have all the tools to *get the job and the life you want.*

This book will, chapter by chapter, step by step, lay out this process, give you examples, and suggest ways of effectively completing each section. It will give you set-up suggestions for your workbook, will refer you to our Web site for ideas and prompts, and will slowly lead you through the process of understanding *where you have gone right.*

You might want to skim through the book once or twice to get a sense of where you are going. However, we encourage you not to jump ahead when you are doing the exercises. In other words, don't try to do the last page first!

It Works—Testimonials

Does this process work? You bet!

The validity of this process is confirmed by the hundreds of individuals who have gone through it over the last 15 years.

Our client list includes recent graduates looking for their first job; 32 year olds getting married, taking on mortgages, having their first child, and wanting to find a job they really love; women returning to the workforce as their children grow up; early retirees still wanting to work and contribute; executives outplaced in their early fifties with lots left in the tank; and lawyers unwilling to commit to 2,200 billable hours at the cost of relationships or health. All have used this process to find new jobs, careers, organizations, and better lives.

Here are some of their comments:

"This isn't just a career assessment program. It is a life assessment program."

"It gives you a set of handrails for life."

"This program gave me the confidence to be myself, not what my parents, teachers, peers thought I should be."

"This program gave me permission to be myself."

"I'm an engineer, an MBA, and I am now teaching grade four and I love it."

"I just didn't feel good about the life I was leading. This program revealed the true me and now I do things I want to do, volunteer in areas I feel I can contribute, and I take time for myself."

"I kept getting involved in things I thought I should get involved in, you know, to be a good citizen. Now I do things I'm good at, and enjoy, and can say no to all those other activities. It is so releasing to know who you are! There are no shoulds!"

"My Mom said I was smart and I could do anything I wanted. She told me not to just be satisfied with being a teacher, a secretary, or a nurse. So I became a geologist, worked in the Arctic and hated it. Now, I teach computers to corporate executives and I love it. I'm a teacher, but not a traditional one. The program helped me understand who I am and what I like doing."

"I was an Olympic gold medallist who was terrified by the real world of jobs. I locked the door to my office. After your program, I went back to school and now I'm a research scientist. I love it. And I'm good at it."

"My brother's a lawyer, my Dad's a lawyer, my grandfather was a judge. I'm supposed to be a lawyer. But, in my soul, I'm not a lawyer. The program gave me confidence to be who I am, and I'm loving my job in sales."

"I'm a grandmother and I started, and ran, one of the most successful independent toy stores in North America. But, I began to hate it. Your program helped me realize why—it's the administration, stupid—so I sold it, and I now lead tours for the elderly. I love it. Thanks."

Commitment and Keeping Track

The previous pages have demonstrated why understanding who you are is vital in choosing *The Right Mountain* for you, professionally and personally. And it has outlined a process to figure this out.

Before going to Everest, I spent nine months of intense physical and mental preparation, three to four hours a day, and up to 8 to 10 hours each day of the weekend.

You have to be prepared to *commit*. You need to decide the priority this process has in your life. We believe it should be your intellectual priority.

Somehow you have to set aside significant, uninterrupted, introspective time. Turn off the cellphone, get away from e-mail, trash the handheld organizer. Try working on this for a minimum of three hours at a time. If you can, work at it twice a day. Give it all the time you can. It is important.

However, it is impossible to be introspective full-time; you need breaks. We've had clients who took no-brainer jobs just to make some money and to have something to do. Others have coached rowing teams, taken salsa dance lessons or philosophy courses, or trained for marathons.

These activities added structure to their lives, and gave them a well-needed break. This structure is especially important for someone who has just been fired, to prevent them from sitting at home brooding.

As we said, you can't go full tilt all the time at anything, so don't *only* do this self-assessment, this introspection. You'll go stir-crazy.

LESSONS FROM EVEREST
You Can't Go Full Tilt All the Time

While in Annapurna, training for Everest, we worked our way up this valley. We would climb up 500 feet then go down 50 feet. Up 1,000 feet. Down 100 feet. Up 1000 feet. Down 50 feet.

We would push ourselves as hard as we could, then ease off, come down a little bit. *You can't go full tilt all the time.* If we kept going up, our bodies might not have acclimatized to the reduction in air pressure and oxygen and we might have become disoriented, confused...and slipped or fallen. And perhaps died. You can't go full tilt at this process either. Take breaks.

This self-assessment process could take you, depending on your age and experiences, 60 to 80 hours. That could be six hours a day, six days a week for two to four weeks, or more. Take your time. *This is the basis for the rest of your life.*

How much time can you set aside, uninterrupted, in a week? What is the priority? You decide. And then commit to it. Set up a schedule and stick to it. No excuses. I knew as I trained for Everest that if once, just once, I skipped a day of training, then I would be able to skip another. So I never let myself miss a single training session—for nine months.

Keeping Track

Before we start to work on the Who Am I? section, let me make a comment on methodology.

You are going to want to keep track of *all* of your thoughts, and you are going to have thoughts and ideas at all hours of the night and day and in a variety of places, including the shower.

To keep track of everything, our clients usually use a three-ring binder. They sometimes handwrite their answers, sometimes type them up on the computer, but they always transfer the ideas into this binder. If they make notes on scraps of paper, they transcribe them onto paper for the binder.

There isn't enough space in this book for you to write your initial responses, let alone subsequent drafts, so we suggest that you don't. By all means, however, underline, highlight, and make notes in the margins! Make this your book!

Never throw anything away. The oddest ideas and comments stimulate new ideas.

In several sections of the guidebook are formats, lists of words, and checklists. You can photocopy them for your binder or go to www.therightmountain.com and print them for your use.

Warnings!

Obviously, you picked up this book because you are looking for help as you make life and/or career decisions. Some of you want more fulfillment in your life, some want more from your job. It doesn't matter what stage you are in. You still have to first know who you are. Will this process help?

As we said, this has helped hundreds before you. But, let me also note what Peter, one of our clients, said, "It is simple. But it is not easy."

Over the 15 years that we have been in practice, we have learned that our process works best for:

1. *Those who are introspective*. If you would like to stop the world for a while and think, digging deep inside yourself, then this process is for you.

2. *Those who can take the time to think*. If you need to make a decision in the next two or three weeks, if you need a paycheck in that time, this may not be for you. How long does it take? I don't know. It is a little like asking how long is a piece of string.

There is no way of knowing, but our experience is that the self-assessment can take 60 to 80 hours.

3. ***Those who understand there is not a specific answer***. If you need to know what specifically you will be doing and where, well, we can't do that. In fact, we don't think anybody can. But that doesn't stop people from wanting it.

Finally, remember, this process works if, and only if, you do the sections in sequence. Don't jump right to values or relationships just because you think they are important. You will only find your *core* through the sequential process in this book.

So, if you'd like to take the time to figure out who you really are, and then take the time to figure out where you'd be happy working and playing, if you'd like to find *The Right Mountain* for you, then you'll love this process.

Ready? Let's start.

WHO AM I?

CHAPTER ONE

Accomplishments

Accomplishments are the basis of everything you will do in this *where have I gone right* process.

Accomplishments are events in your life that gave you a sense of real satisfaction.

They need not be world-changing events. In fact, they hardly ever will be. You'll probably have to do some digging to find them. In many cases, they will be events that you take little notice of because you think of them as *normal*, as situations in which you used your *common sense*, so they're no big deal.

Many people, especially our younger clients, plead that they haven't accomplished anything yet, and they say this lack of having done anything is, in fact, the problem.

Not so. We all have accomplishments! Quit looking for the huge, change-the-world things. Instead, look for those times when you felt good after you successfully followed a recipe, threw a party, polished a car until it was showroom-bright, helped a little brother learn to catch a ball, found just that perfect dress for the dance, made a school team, got the part in a play, lost weight, got in shape, went back to school in mid-life to take courses that interested you, rebuilt a relationship with an unhappy customer, organized your financial affairs, managed or coached your child's little league team. Little things. But things that gave you satisfaction. These are all accomplishments. Each accomplishment, each event will, must, be set up as follows:

1. a *problem*, an issue, or an opportunity,

2. the *action* you took to resolve it, and

3. a *result* that made you feel good.

We call this set-up **PAR**: problem, action, result.

To catalogue these events, we ask you to look at the five main aspects of your life—education, work experience, extra-curricular activity, volunteer activity, and personal time. This breakdown is totally arbitrary. There may be crossover between categories. No problem. The goal is to get a broad range of accomplishments, to ensure that we have covered everything and not missed anything important. Start making a list in summary form, set up as PARs— problem, action, result—just to get you started. You can fill in the details later.

How do you find accomplishments? There is no simple way, especially if your formal education and extracurricular activities were years ago, or if you think you are too young to have really accomplished anything.

Some of our clients use diaries; others use photo albums, where they linger over photos trying to recreate the event or situation. Others use high school and college yearbooks. Some ask parents or friends if they remember any time that they had a huge smile on their face. Many reflect on the stories, the anecdotes, they repeat time after time. These usually describe the things in life they love to do, their accomplishments.

Usually it comes from in-depth probing of yourself, relentlessly digging into times at school, at camp, at work, or volunteering.

Sometimes we remember instances on a trip, or at the office, when we just felt good.

The answers tend to come after hours of solitary introspection. You think of something, it leads to something else, and then up pops an event that you remember with real joy. Often no one else even knew it happened. What kind of things?

Well, here are some examples from my own self-assessment workbook. I have tightened them up to simplify them. Remember, your write-ups can start out one, two, or three pages long. Eventually, when we get to the résumé stage, you will do a précis of them.

1. **Problem**: Bobby was terrified of the water and wasn't going to go near it. But to participate in camp activities— sailing, canoeing, swimming—he had to swim.

   Action: As his camp counselor, I thought I had four options:

   - Go to the Camp Director, a psychiatrist

   - Go to the Waterfront Director, presumably an expert at getting kids to swim

   - Ask my Section Director to transfer Bobby to a more experienced counselor

   - Figure out, on my own, how to get him to swim

      I decided to do it myself.

      I took him to the beach, dug canals in the sand, played with minnows, splashed water. Then we threw sticks into the lake for the camp dog to fetch. Sometimes the dog got bored with the game, and I'd ask Bobby to get the stick. Unthinking, he'd go into the water, and sometimes have to wrestle the dog for the stick. He got comfortable in the water.

      Eventually he swam, he sailed, and he played water polo.

At the end of camp, he hugged me and said thanks.

Result: I'd made a difference, helped conquer a fear, and created a way to help Bobby. I listened, I understood, I empathized, and I found my own solution, independently, to the problem.

2. **Problem**: I had severely injured my back and my movement was restricted.

All my friends were going to the mountains for a ski holiday at Christmas, and I wanted to be with them. I took a couple of ski lessons at our local hill, but my back screamed in agony when I tried to carve turns the way my instructor told me to. The normal ski techniques wouldn't work for me. The demands of shifting weight, and digging in my skis to turn, were too much for my weak back.

Action: I decided that I understood the principles of turning, but I would have to create my own style. Every day I practiced for hours, first on small hills, and gradually on bigger and bigger slopes. Finally I created a technique that worked, and didn't hurt me.

Result: It wasn't pretty, and I didn't look like everyone else, but it worked. I could ski all the hills with them, and I had a ball on that Christmas ski holiday.

3. **Problem**: I was a traveling salesman, and one store on my route refused to talk to me or even let me on the property.

Action: On my third visit, I confronted the manager and asked for 30 seconds of his time. He refused.

On the fourth and fifth visits, he continued to refuse to give me 30 seconds. On the sixth he finally relented.

I asked him why he wouldn't let me sell him our product line, which had three brands that were number one in their categories.

He said it was because my predecessor had not given him a $20 display allowance that he had promised to pay.

I offered him $20 from my pocket. He refused it, saying he wanted a check from my company to prove that they recognized the obligation.

It took me weeks of cajoling my manager and the bureaucracy because there was no proof of performance, but I finally got the check.

Result: I returned to his store, gave him the check, and sold him a minimum case order! Business picked up with each successive call.

4. **Problem**: I volunteered to be on the board of a local charity, but was soon overwhelmed by the inertia that 40 board members created at every meeting.

Action: Rather than quit, I looked for others who were obviously frustrated by the same issue, and created an ad hoc committee of three. I suggested we focus on an issue that the board had tabled, and I created a process to find a solution.

Result: We found a solution and I presented it to the board. They accepted it, and it made a real difference.

You see, not big earth-shaking events, but stuff where I felt really good, really satisfied. Times where I had gone right. Accomplishments.

Accomplishments Versus Common Sense

Some of you will say that these events are not accomplishments but are, in fact, just uses of my common sense. That's right. They are common-sense acts that came naturally to me. But, that doesn't mean that they aren't accomplishments. In fact, it makes sense that you would want to do a job that is "common sense" to you, doesn't it? Because then you will do it well…and easily. And you will be successful.

As an aside, we don't believe there is any such thing as "common sense." I have a power lawnmower, and when it doesn't work I take it to a mechanic (usually after staring at it for a while, and sometimes kicking it to see if that will help it to start). My neighbor Bill looks at me when I tell him that I've just paid $50 to get it started and says, "But Jim, it's just common sense. You start at the gas tank, see if there is gas, follow it through the gas line to the carburetor, to the spark plugs, to the…(and here, I tune out). You just see where the problem is, and fix it. It's just common sense."

To him, it is. But not to me.

On the other hand, he and I drive to work together occasionally. He's an engineer who runs a team that builds subway stations. He once told me he was having trouble getting his staff to do what he wanted them to do. I asked him how he worked with them. He said, "I tell them what I want them to do, and I expect them to do it." I asked if he ever listens to their comments or problems. He said, "No. They have a job to do and they should just do it." I suggested that dealing with people effectively entails listening and understanding. It's just common sense.

To me it is. But not to him.

Bill's common sense and my common sense are different!

That's why we think there is no such thing as "common sense." Perhaps we really should use the term "individual sense."

Identifying Accomplishments

Identifying accomplishments can be very difficult. You look at activities and see no real accomplishment. It was just common sense to you. It was easy.

It is these "easy" things that we want to find, so we can replicate them and make your job easy; thus, satisfying; thus, motivating. Thus, you will be…here we go again…successful.

Many accomplishments may not even be noticeable to others:

- Moving a school mark from "D" to "B"

- Helping a child catch a frog in a swamp

- Throwing a great stag party for a friend

- Winning a part in a play

- Getting a summer job

- Learning the names of customers on your paper route

- Helping a co-worker overcome a problem

- Confronting your child on a difficult issue

- Helping a friend choose a dress for her wedding

- Saying no when everyone else is saying yes

- Getting others to join a neighborhood watch group

- Helping your child overcome a fear

In each case, there was a problem, an issue, an opportunity. In each case, you did something, even if it was a "common sense" action. You figured out an approach and then you just did it. In each case, you felt you had accomplished something, if not then, at least now, as you look back at it.

We are looking for accomplishments in the whole spectrum of your life. And, we are looking for enough accomplishments to help us find patterns.

We are looking for at least four accomplishments in each of these five categories:

1. Education: all levels, including evening classes and courses for your job

2. Work: part-time or full-time

3. Extra-curricular: this is where you get involved with others, in an informal way—playing golf, sailing, going to clubs, playing on school teams, acting in plays

4. Volunteer: non-paying organized programs to assist others, such as coaching, fundraising, publicizing bake sales, being a Big Sister, service clubs

5. Personal: these may be hobbies, exercise programs, music collections, etc.

(Categories 3 and 5 obviously can overlap.)

Take your time. Dig deep. Think back to times at school, on the job, everywhere. Make lists of possible accomplishments before you try to write them out in full. Or, if it works better for you, write some out in full to see how it feels. Find a method that works for you.

Regardless of how you do it, remember that the set-up is PAR:

• *Problem*/issue/opportunity

• Your *action*

• The *result*, why it felt good

Overwhelmed? Then think of the Everest climb I took part in. It was certainly overwhelming. Remember how the team handled the challenge? We took it one step at a time.

LESSONS FROM EVEREST
One Step at a Time

From Base Camp, it is still 10 miles horizontally to a line drawn down vertically from the peak. And it is 12,028 feet, over two miles vertically, to the peak.

Overwhelmed? You bet. But we kept going, step by step, because we knew how important our goal was. This process is important to you, isn't it?

This is going to take time and effort. Your friends and family are going to ask you what you are doing, and why it takes so long. Ask for their support before you start. Get them to buy into it with you. Ask them to commit, as you are committing.

Overwhelmed? How did others do it? Here's what they say:

1. Start slowly, look at one category at a time. If you find nothing at first, try another category. Then come back to the first one. There is no right way.

2. The accomplishments may start out as just a phrase or a paragraph, or they may be several pages long. There is no standard, no limit.

3. Eventually you may have three accomplishments in some categories and five in others. That's fine. Having only one or two in a category is not acceptable.

4. Set up your workbook/binder so there is a separate page (or pages) for each accomplishment. Here is a suggested set-up for each accomplishment. If it will help, go to our Web site, www.therightmountain.com, for this set-up.

Category _____

Accomplishment # _____

Title _____

Problem/Issue/Opportunity _____

_____

What I did/Actions I took: _____

_____

Result that made me feel good, and why: _____

_____

Use this set-up, or something like it, for all 20 accomplishments.

While you are digging, you will probably discover events in school or work that you were forced to do, and did well, but you didn't enjoy. You don't consider them to be accomplishments in your terms. Make a note of them. As our client Maggie said, she did a lot of thinking about things she had to do but didn't like, and she used these to fend off job offers that were not a good fit. She also found them to be useful in identifying things she was not good at. Food for thought.

Dig deep. It is worth it. It can be a long, laborious process. It is not easy. No one, who has done our program or used this process, including me, has found this to be easy. When I found the going particularly difficult, when I was sick and tired of it, and felt I had run out of accomplishments at 12, I remembered an incident from my first full-time job.

As I said earlier, I was a traveling salesman for Procter & Gamble. My territory was the interior of British Columbia, Canada. It was huge. I drove 1,200 miles a week. And when I took it over no one had worked it for over a year, so there was no list of stores, no suggested routes, nothing to help me. I bought a map and started driving town to town.

One day as I was driving, I glanced at the map and saw a town about 50 miles to the west, Lillooet, and thought that I should go there.

I started up a one-lane, gravel road, with steep drops to the left of several hundred feet into the Fraser River. It was a difficult drive, made unthinkable by the appearance of huge logging trucks coming the other way. Several times I had to back up over half a mile to a lay-by, so a truck could pass. They certainly weren't going to back up!

Four harrowing hours later I arrived in Lillooet, a one-street town with four small stores that might carry my products. I went into the first one, a Chinese grocery store.

I introduced myself.

"Hi, I'm Jim Hayhurst with Procter & Gamble: Crest, Duncan Hines, Crisco."

"What you doing here?" asked the Chinese gentleman behind the counter, obviously surprised to see me.

"I've come to sell you these great products, number one in their respective categories."

"What you doing here today? How you get here?" he said with a heavy accent.

"I drove up the road. How else could I get here?"

"Salesmen come by train, only on Tuesdays. No one use road."

I could understand why, having just driven it, but, now that I was here, I wanted to sell and then get out of town before it got dark.

"You go see other stores, then come back see me. We talk then."

I went to the other three stores—a drugstore, a butcher shop, and a dry goods store. I didn't sell much. They didn't seem to be selling much. The town seemed deserted. I went back to the Chinese grocery store.

"Come. Have tea. How much you sell?" We walked through the bead curtains to his kitchen.

"Not much, there doesn't seem to be much going on here. I've driven all this way and I haven't even sold enough to put together a minimum case order. This has not been an easy day. And I still have to drive back down that road."

The man looked at me with a small grin on his face. "Who ever said…was going to be…easy?"

I have never forgotten that question.

Who ever said…was going to be…easy?

There are all kinds of comparable phrases, such as "nothing worthwhile ever comes without effort," but my grocer put it so succinctly.

This is tough. It takes work. My business partner, Chris, when he was working through this book, said he kept coming up with accomplishments, but they always had a "but" at the end.

"I created a model for analyzing marketing problems, but…it didn't work for everyone."

"I now have a great relationship with my eldest daughter, but…it took me 10 years."

"I had my golf handicap down to four, but…it has crept up to seven."

Forget the *buts*, or as my lady friend Liz says, "The *but* stops here."

Chris created the model, built the relationship, got his handicap down to four. These were all real accomplishments. What skills did he use, what were the interest areas, what were the values inherent in each accomplishment? These were truly times where he had gone right.

It is not easy, but, *who ever said it was going to be easy?*

It is, however, worthwhile.

All of us, including me, look back on successful completion of this process as one of the most satisfying and rewarding accomplishments of our lives. It changed our lives.

It is perhaps interesting to note here, as Chris pointed out to me, that all of this book is based on positives, on accomplishments, on where we have gone right, rather than on negatives. Most therapy work, it seems, is based on the negatives. It suggests that everything mentioned before the **but** in a sentence should be discounted. We are not psychologists, nor are we therapists, and if there are issues in these areas we do not pretend to have the answers. But we do believe in focusing on the positive, on the **right** stuff in our lives, so we can ensure more *right* stuff in our future.

LESSONS FROM EVEREST
Who Ever Said It Was Going to Be Easy?

The Right Mountain journey is a long process. It is not easy, but it is worthwhile.

CHAPTER TWO

Skills

Now that you have your list of accomplishments, are feeling good about them, and have taken them as far as you can, you can move on to the next step. You are going to break these accomplishments down by the *Skills* you used in achieving them.

Most of us do not give ourselves credit for the skills we have. We often think these skills are really just common sense. But, as we learned earlier, there is no such thing as common sense. Bill's common sense about engines makes no sense to me. And my common sense about people makes no sense to him.

This section, therefore, is going to *tease* out those skills that you take for granted.

There are, it turns out, three categories of skills:

1. **Functional**

    These are skills that are relevant to your interaction with people, data, or things. Functional skills include words such as assembled, computed, designed, installed, organized, and selected.

2. **Personality**
   These are relatively consistent patterns of behavior and, while learnable, are usually most useful if they come naturally. These skills include words such as adaptable, dependable, persistent, and self-starter.

3. **Knowledge**
   These are skills that are learned and applied to specific situations. These include words such as accounting, welding, scuba diving, and computer programming.

In a moment we will provide you with lists of functional and personality skills. You may decide to type the lists on your computer. Or, as we said earlier, go to www.therightmountain.com and print the lists from there. No problem. We do suggest that you use a separate skills list for each accomplishment to ensure that you analyze each event individually. Clients who have used one list seem to get mesmorized and just keep noting the same skill over and over again.

We have also learned that it is important to have a specific definition of these skill words. It almost doesn't matter what the definition is—just be sure you use it consistently. For example, some may think *aggressive* is bad because it means dominating, while others think it is good because it helps overcome problems on the way to accomplishments. Choose a definition that works for you. We will never have a definitive list, so feel free to add words.

We do not list knowledge skills because that list could be endless. You will know if you have a particular knowledge skill as a result of a specific educational or training program. Interestingly, most of us have very few knowledge skills, so don't be embarrassed if you don't have many.

Take your 20 accomplishments and, using the functional skills list on the following page, check off the ones that are apparent in each individual accomplishment. Take your time, think logically through the accomplishment, don't skip common sense skills ("well, of course you do that"); go back and review the list. There can never be too many, and you may find that you used 10, 15, or 22 skills in an individual accomplishment. That's great! Don't be so surprised. You do have skills! Now do the same for the personality skills list. It is a long and sometimes tedious process, but it helps you realize all the skills you have.

Now, go back through the accomplishments and see if any knowledge skills were used. As we said, don't be surprised if this list is very short. Most of us do not have a large base of true *knowledge* skills, skills that have a proven technical basis for their application, such as medicine, astronomy, or the professions in general.

FUNCTIONAL SKILLS LIST

Achieve		Examine		Motivate	
Acquire		Execute		Negotiate	
Adjust		Expand		Observe	
Administer		Expedite		Organize	
Analyze		Explain		Perceive	
Arrange		Facilitate		Perform	
Assemble		Finalize		Persuade	
Build		Forecast		Plan	
Buy		Foster		Prepare	
Clarify		Generate		Present	
Classify		Help		Prioritize	
Coach		Hire		Program	
Communicate		Implement		Prove	
Compare		Improve		Question	
Compile		Increase		Recommend	
Compose		Influence		Reconcile	
Conduct		Inform		Recruit	
Consult		Initiate		Renovate	
Coordinate		Install		Repair	
Counsel		Instruct		Report	
Create		Interpret		Research	
Debate		Interview		Review	
Decide		Invent		Revise	
Define		Investigate		Schedule	
Delegate		Launch		Select	
Design		Lead		Sell	
Develop		Listen		Stimulate	
Direct		Maintain		Summarize	
Encourage		Manage		Teach	
Enlist		Mediate		Train	
Establish		Memorize		Translate	
Evaluate		Monitor		Write	

PERSONALITY SKILLS LIST

Adaptable		Easygoing		Opportunistic	
Add Value		Efficient		Optimistic	
Adventurous		Empathetic		Organized	
Aggressive		Energetic		Persistent	
Ambitious		Enthusiastic		Practical	
Argumentative		Firm		Praising	
Assertive		Flexible		Relaxed	
Calm		Fun		Responsible	
Caring		Fussy		Risk Taker	
Cautious		Humorous		Serious	
Competitive		Idealistic		Sociable	
Confident		Imaginative		Spendthrift	
Cooperative		Independent		Systematic	
Courageous		Inspiring		Tactful	
Creative		Intuitive		Talkative	
Curious		Inventive		Thoughtful	
Decisive		Kind		Tolerant	
Dedicated		Loyal		Tough	
Determined		Moody		Trusting	

Once you feel you have completely listed all the skills used in each of the accomplishments, add up the number of times you used each skill. Take a clean list of skills, and put this total beside each word. This will give you a sense of how skillful you truly are. Congratulations! Are you surprised? You shouldn't be. You do have, and use, skills.

You'll end up with a list that probably doesn't include all the skill words—some simply aren't *individual sense* to you—and you'll see that some skills are used much more frequently than others. The ones that occur most often are your Core Skills, and the relative number of times they appear will be an insight into their priority.

One of the skills that few of us are taught is prioritization, yet it is a vital skill in life. And it is a vital skill in getting the most out of this process. Why? Let me illustrate.

In our one-on-one program, I often use the example of the owner of a small clothing store. She wants to go on a holiday, and has recruited a friend to look after the store. Just before the owner leaves, her friend asks if she has any last-minute words of advice if customers come in with complaints. The owner thinks about it, and says that she has two priorities:

1. Making sales and getting cash, because business is slow and she has to pay the rent.

2. Customer satisfaction, because that means they will come back, and probably bring their friends.

The friend thinks about this and asks, "What if a customer comes in to return a dress because the zipper has broken? What do I do then? Do I tell her I'm sorry, I don't know how she broke it but we can't do anything about it (that saves us the cost of getting it repaired), or tell her we'll fix it or offer her a replacement (that keeps her satisfied)?

Which do I do? Which is the first priority? Save the cash or satisfy the customer?"

*You can't have two **first** priorities*. You must decide.

In life, you have to set priorities. You are unlikely to find a fully equipped car at a low price, or a house in the ideal neighborhood at a low price. You have to decide if cost, or features or location, is number one. It is difficult to do. But you have to do it.

Take the lists of functional and personality skills on which you have noted the number of times they appear; e.g., functional skills:

Analyze	20
Research	20
Communicate	18
Facilitate	14
Help	18
Motivate	14
Organize	14
Lead	12

The numbers on this list may not be the true prioritization, but it is a start. You may decide that while you used a particular skill most frequently, it is not the skill you like to use the most.

Now list the top five functional and personality skills, in order of priority for you, based on your satisfaction in using that skill, e.g., I like motivating better than analyzing.

Let me use my skill lists as an example.

The functional skills I noted in teaching Bobby how to swim were:

Analyze	Explain	Listen
Challenge	Facilitate	Motivate
Coach	Foster	Observe
Communicate	Help	Perceive
Create	Implement	Persuade
Decide	Influence	Plan
Design	Initiate	Stimulate
Encourage	Lead	Supervise

From my original workbook, I found that the top 10 functional skills I had used in my 20 accomplishments were:

Motivate	20	Help	16
Communicate	20	Create	16
Persuade	19	Encourage	15
Listen	18	Analyze	14
Coach	18	Observe	12

When I prioritized them based on what I really liked to do most of all, my top five functional skills were:

1. Communicate

2. Motivate

3. Listen

4. Coach

5. Encourage

After doing the same work on personality skills, my top five, in order of priority, were:

1. Independent

2. Caring

3. Enthusiastic

4. Energetic

5. Inspiring

Once you know the priority of these skills, it makes your life, your goals, and your accomplishments so much easier to understand.

It's funny, most of us don't think of words such as *dependable*, *persistent*, *assemble*, or *install* as skills, but indeed they are. You can imagine how much an employer wants a *dependable* staff member!

These are the skills we want to use again and again in our jobs, in our careers, in our lives to be successful. And the good news is that each of us has different skills, thank goodness, or we would all want to do the same thing.

LESSONS FROM EVEREST
We Each Have Different Skills

Everyone has a role, but it must be both comfortable and accepted by the individual and the team. The key is to understand what you and each of the others does best, and maximize those skills at the appropriate opportunities.

CHAPTER THREE

Interests

Your involvement—your commitment, either professionally or personally—is going to be greatest if you are interested. And, not surprisingly, you will apply your Core Skills most effectively in areas that interest you.

So, what are *Interest Areas*?

Simply speaking, interest areas can be divided into three categories:

1. *People*—activities with other people. People are the main reason for doing whatever it may be. If you play bridge to be with people, rather than for the strategy of the game, then it is a people interest.

2. *Data*—thinking activities, such as researching, programming, discussing philosophy, spirituality, or reading—and playing bridge. If you are most interested in the mental—the strategic part of the game—then the activity is a data interest.

3. *Things*—physical activities where the focus is on doing. Few people probably play bridge for the card holding, or the shuffling excitement, so bridge won't often end up here.

Watch out! The same activity (such as bridge) can end up in one, two, or even three categories depending on how you view it. Tennis, for example, can be categorized under:

1. *People*—you play primarily for the social aspect, because you like being with friends.

2. *Data*—you are most interested in the technical aspects of the equipment, or the strategy of the game.

3. *Things*—you play for the doing, the physical aspect, to work up a sweat, or for the adrenaline rush.

Think about why you do the activity so you can see where it fits.

On Everest, the interest areas varied considerably by climber.

Jimmy's interest area was people.

Some were interested in physical things.

Data, such as the height climbed or the oxygen level, was important to others.

Almost universally, one of these categories is dominant in each of us. In order to determine the area of emphasis for you, we suggest the following exercise be completed in your workbook. Go back to your accomplishments summary and look for examples and insights.

1. *People*

   - Make a list of six or more activities you enjoy doing with people, family, friends, work associates (e.g., going to movies, golf, holding dinner parties, walking on the beach).

   - What are the common elements in these activities? List them (e.g., small groups, laughter, competition).

2. *Data*

   - Make a list of six or more activities that you enjoy doing with data, knowledge, or information (e.g., thinking activities, such as computer games, crossword puzzles, reading, discussions, your spirituality, debating).

   - What are the common elements in these activities? List them (e.g., logical thinking, testing your memory, extrapolating, organizing your thoughts, arguments).

3. *Things*

   - Make a list of six or more physical activities that you enjoy doing with things (e.g., building models, decorating a room, growing your own vegetables).

   - What are the common elements in these activities? List them (e.g., being by myself, doing something concrete).

If you think prioritization is important, and obviously we do, and if you would like to improve your prioritization skills, we suggest you rank the lists within each category.

LESSONS FROM EVEREST
Prioritization Is Important

We can't carry everything up the mountain. Our ability to prioritize and take the right equipment might save our lives.

Of all the interests that you have listed, summarize the ones that give you the greatest sense of satisfaction, that you like doing the most.

Which of the people, data, or things lists came most easily to you? Which gave you the most enjoyment? These answers indicate your *Core Interest Area*, be it people, data, or things. It doesn't necessarily mean you aren't interested in the other areas, just that one is your focus. This is the interest area that you should ensure is a major part of your job. My Core Interest, as you can see, is people, so my job and my life should always involve people.

CHAPTER FOUR

Values

Values are the most underrated, underutilized, misunderstood, but most important element of our being.

I don't know where we get values, but, in all our work with clients, it is apparent that our Core Values are a constant from our early years. Maybe we get them in the birth canal, I don't know. Many people think they evolve, but our experience is that they don't change.

I do know that once we get into interactive life, in families, in neighborhoods, in schools, and in jobs, we start to get other values layered on us by our parents, our teachers, our coaches, our peers, and our society. And we lose track of who we really are as we start to accept these other value words as our own.

Money, prestige, status, cars, houses, keeping up with the neighbors all become valued by us. But they may not be our own values. And we become confused, disillusioned, lost.

We often hear older people say, "If I knew then what I know now, I'd have done it differently." They are getting back to their Core Values with the experience of age.

On their deathbed, you *never* hear people say, "I wish I'd spent more time at the office." They seem, at this point in time, to wish they'd spent more time with their family, paid more attention to their own health, or maintained their integrity, their *Core* Values.

"Too soon old, too late smart" is their lament.

Implicit in the definition of values, we believe, is that some action on your part is required to achieve or maintain them. Values may not be readily apparent, or what we think they are. Our client Maggie found that "looking for things I could not live without" was useful. "What if I had to live away from my friends, my family, my money, my freedom? When the thought of losing something gave me the most gut-wrenching feeling, then I knew it was an important value." They seem to be guiding principles.

She also found writing down values in her present environment useful. She wrote down her parent's values, Polish values (her heritage), Canadian values (she grew up in Canada), and Saudi Arabian values (she worked there), just to get perspective. It was a useful exercise to see where she had adopted values from her environment that were not really her own.

This section is an attempt to ensure that you have the understanding of your Core Values, so you can make better life decisions.

Let me give you some case histories of how values come into play.

1. Tex started delivering newspapers at 8, had a Christmas tree lot at 14, sold motorcycles at 16, and had his own motorcycle store in college (he was making more money than the college president). He went into real estate and then the land development business. He was driven by money. He thought his Core Value was money. But when he came up against a true challenge, he learned differently. Tex was hit by cancer in his early fifties. His money didn't make much of a difference, but he soon learned how much his family meant to him. As he lived with his cancer, family became, and until his death was, the cornerstone of his life.

   Family was his Core Value.

2. Chris thought he was a risk taker, an entrepreneur. He had helped start new businesses, had led turnarounds, and was a creative out-of-the-box thinker. He decided to buy a successful business and, with his strategic skills, build it exponentially. He kept looking at businesses, but never closed a purchase. He wondered why. After a review of his values, it turned out he was much more security conscious than he thought. He would never risk a significant portion of his wealth and thus he couldn't afford to buy a truly successful business. And, he realized, he had always worked with a partner. Independence, autonomy, and risk were, in fact, low on his prioritized list of values.

   Security was his Core Value.

3. Megan tells me she always believed that she wanted to be a leader in her field, whatever it might be. She wanted prestige, status, power. She wasn't sure which was number one, but it was one of those without a doubt. She got her BA and her MA, worked for a while, and then went back to get her law degree. When it came time to get a job, her excellent scholastic record meant that the top law firms were courting her with promises of eventual partnerships and chances to head up specific practice areas. It was then, when confronted with these options and these decisions, that she realized that she didn't want to be at the top of the ladder; she wasn't even sure she wanted to be a partner. She wanted time for a family, and a lifestyle that was not available in the big firm or, probably, in the big city. She believed she would likely be happier in a small town and small firm, with a more nine-to-five job than a workaholic environment.

   She realized her values were more in the area of personal growth, family, and community.

4. Peter had a growing construction business, a wife, and two fun kids, and the future looked bright. He came to us because he had developed an allergy that reacted to virtually everything on

the construction site: dust, sawdust, glue, etc. He had to find a new career. To complicate matters, he had just bought a bigger house and had a bigger mortgage. To further complicate matters, his wife's sister had just gone through a difficult divorce, and, because she had no money, had moved into their house with her two kids. So, he needed to make big money to support his "two wives and four kids." His Core Value he said was, and indeed he thought always had been, money or wealth. He thought they were the same. While we don't usually suggest job opportunities to our clients, I had just met with a friend who had returned from Saudi Arabia desperately searching for project managers to build a telephone installation. I thought Peter would be perfect. The fact that he knew the construction business but wouldn't have to be on-site and therefore wouldn't have allergic reactions, was perfect. And the pay? He would net about $175,000 plus bonus, and have a cost-of-living allowance and free travel for his family. I told him about it. Fabulous! He said he'd go home and talk to his "wives."

He came back the next day, dejected. He'd gone home full of hope and enthusiasm at this great solution to his career crisis and, after much discussion, had realized that his Core Value, his driving motivation, wasn't money. As they talked about the opportunity, Peter, his wife, and his sister-in-law all realized that they couldn't leave their hometown. Peter's mother had recently passed away, leaving his father alone. While in good health, his only support system was Peter and his family, especially the grandchildren. If they moved to Saudi Arabia, he would probably not survive the loneliness.

Family was Peter's Core Value. He couldn't take the job, even though it satisfied the money need—his apparent Core Value. However, the good news was that this opportunity, combined with the insights our program had revealed, enabled Peter to sell himself into a project manager office job for a condominium builder in his local area. He had found a job, one consistent with his Core Values.

Here is a list of value words. To list is to omit, so feel free to add any words you feel are appropriate and important to you. We suggest you either photocopy this for your binder, type it into your computer so you can start to prioritize these critical elements of your being, or, as before, print the list from www.theright-mountain.com.

VALUES LIST

Adding Value		Health		Prestige	
Advancement		Helping Others		Reputation	
Authority		Humility		Respect	
Autonomy		Income—Commission		Responsibility	
Camaraderie		Income—Salary		Risk	
Challenge		Independence		Satisfaction	
Community		Integrity		Security	
Connection		Leadership		Stability	
Contribution to Society		Leisure Time		Status	
Control		Merit		Tradition	
Courage		Personal Growth		Variety	
Family		Personal Relationship		Wealth	
Fun		Power		Other (list)	

Write a definition for each word to ensure that you are consistent in your evaluation of it, so you know exactly what you mean by status, family, independence, or fun.

Now, take your time and note the relative importance of each of these words to you on a 1–10 scale (with 10 being the highest). Here it is difficult to separate work and personal life, so don't try. Make a first try at the list. Then stop. Leave it for a while, then come back. Massage the relative importance until you feel comfortable.

Now, take the six values that you have ranked highest. Write an explanation for these selections. Obviously there is no right or wrong answer, but your accomplishments should give you some indication why these are important to you.

It is often interesting to note the values you ranked lowest, and understand the reasons why. Try writing an explanation for these also. It may give you some insights.

Review the top six, test them, prioritize them, and then live with them for a little while. Try using them in day-to-day decision-making. Move the priorities around if necessary. Look for new words. It will take time for them to settle into order, and for you to feel comfortable and confident with them. We have clients who tape the list to the bathroom mirror, refrigerator, or car dash, just so they can keep noodling their relative importance.

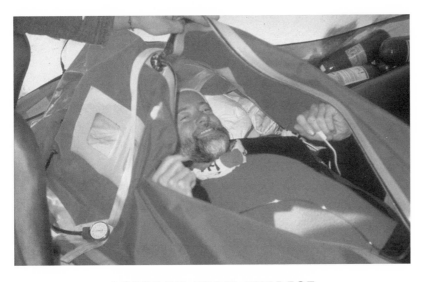

LESSONS FROM EVEREST
Understanding Your Core Values
Will Help You Make Decisions Easier

In life and death situations, your Core Values often become vividly apparent. Rick, one of our team members at Everest, got pulmonary edema and would have died had we not been able to put him in this pressurized Gamow bag. I realized that it could easily have been me in the bag. And I used my Core Values, control of my destiny and family, to help me make the decision, to turn back when I got the first signs of cerebral edema. And I turned back without regret.

Relationships

Unless you plan to be a hermit, or live on a desert island, you will probably be around people. And you will form *relationships* with them.

In your personal life you choose friends whom you are compatible with, make a connection with. You naturally go to people who have the same interests, perhaps the same skills and certainly the same values as you have.

So when you are looking for a job, deciding whether or not to join a certain organization, wouldn't it be great if you could imagine developing *relationships* with these people too? To do this, you need to understand the characteristics of people you relate well with and to, and then you test your potential associates against these criteria.

Sometimes this list will reveal why you had trouble with a co-worker or boss in previous jobs or volunteer activities. Sometimes it is as simple as a difference in ambition, the fact that they weren't organized or that they were sarcastic. These are simple, perhaps even little things, but they become annoying and affect your performance and level of satisfaction.

A cowboy will tell you that the smallest burr under the saddle blanket on a horse can, over the course of a day's ride, cripple a horse. It is tiny, but it rubs and rubs so that eventually the horse tries to compensate for the soreness. He changes his natural gait, contorts himself.

It is the same with people. Someone rubs us the wrong way and soon it seems to happen more and more often. Eventually it affects everything we do and it changes our natural gait, our normal way of doing things. We contort ourselves and diminish our effectiveness.

What are the characteristics of the people you are most comfortable and most productive with?

In this section of your workbook, list the personal characteristics of people you enjoy associating with, either at work or in social situations. Again, go back to your list of accomplishments for insights into the people you were successful with.

Then, and only after you have made this list, look at the characteristics in the following list (this list is also on www.-therightmountain.com).

Using this list and your own list, note the 10 most important and 10 least important characteristics of people you enjoy being with. Prioritize the top five.

This list will be a guide to help you ensure the best chance for developing good, productive relationships.

Before you accept a job or volunteer offer, ask if you can meet some of the people you will be working with and for. Meet as many as you can. Use your list of characteristics, both important and not important, to check out their compatibility with you.

Relationships are probably not the most important criteria in accepting a position. Your skills, interests, and values are more important. But they can help make a decision when it is a flip of the coin.

And if you go into a job or volunteer position knowing that there will be some conflicts with the characteristics of some of your new associates, you can control your reactions, behaviors and expectations, thus reducing stress and anxiety. Thus you improve your chances of feeling good in your new role…and your life.

CHARACTERISTICS LIST

Adaptable		Energetic		Organized	
Adventurous		Enthusiastic		Outspoken	
Aggressive		Firm		Patient	
Ambitious		Flexible		Persistent	
Argumentative		Forgetful		Practical	
Assertive		Fun		Praising	
Boastful		Fussy		Relaxed	
Calm		Humorous		Responsible	
Caring		Idealistic		Sarcastic	
Cautious		Imaginative		Serious	
Competitive		Independent		Sociable	
Confident		Intuitive		Thrifty	
Cooperative		Inventive		Systematic	
Curious		Kind		Tactful	
Decisive		Loyal		Talkative	
Dominant		Methodical		Tolerant	
Easygoing		Moody		Tough	
Efficient		Opportunistic		Trusting	
Empathetic		Optimistic		Wary	

Core Accomplishments

This is a review, and if necessary, a revision section.

You have listed your accomplishments, and teased out your skills, interests, values, and relationships. You have boiled all of these down to the core: to the Core Skills, Core Interests, Core Values, and priority relationship characteristics.

Now, you want to review the accomplishments you detailed in the first section, and see if they really are demonstrations or proof of your Core Skills, Core Interests, and Core Values. You want to see if they really utilized these cores and if they, in retrospect, are *Core Accomplishments*.

When I drafted my accomplishments in the first section, I included one when I was Head of the Counselor-in-Training section at a summer camp. I had forty-eight 18-year-old boys working for me, and I was only 21. Every day I had to allocate 136 jobs at the camp to these guys. I had a big board filled with their names, the jobs, and the times they were required. My job was recognized as the top job in camp, and I was thrilled to have it. And I got praise for the great job I was doing. I wrote it up as a real accomplishment.

But when I got to this Core Accomplishment Section and looked at this accomplishment relative to my Core Skills, Interests, and Values, I realized that there wasn't a match. My core functional skills are communicating, motivating, listening, coaching, and encouraging but my job had no time for these. I just allocated almost faceless people to an ever-increasing list of tasks. My core personality skills are independent, caring, enthusiastic, energetic, inspiring, and I certainly wasn't using these skills standing at the job board. My Core Interest area was people, but dawn to dusk, I was at the job board; I didn't spend any time with the actual people.

I thought it was an accomplishment but, in fact, it wasn't. The real accomplishment was, I think, getting the job, because I had beaten out three other really good guys, and having the job, because it had prestige and status. But these did not match my Core Values of independence and making a difference. It was not a Core Accomplishment, but merely a response to my love of challenge, a value I ended up putting well down the list.

But I loved camp. Surely, there was something there that was a Core Accomplishment. I kept looking. Then I remembered Bobby. I told you a bit about him in Chapter One. Bobby, in fact, was a Core Accomplishment. Let me set the scene.

The first day of summer camp, the kids arrived tired, scared, and lonely after a long bus trip. They all wore tags that indicated their name, cabin number, and a color corresponding to their section (mine was blue).

As a counselor, my job was to find the kids allocated to my cabin as they got off the bus. So I looked for kids with blue tags and the number two (my cabin), and welcomed them by name. I was 18 and my campers were 12 years old. When I found one of my kids, I would take him to my section and settle him into the cabin.

A little blond kid got off the bus, blue tag, number two, and his name was Bobby. I scampered over, put my hand out and said, "Hi, Bobby! I'm Hurst (my nickname), I'm your Counselor. Let's go to the cabin and choose a great bed."

He looked up at me, crossed his arms over his chest, and said, "I'm not going to swim this summer."

"Look at the lake Bobby, it's beautiful and it's warmer than ever before. You'll love it. Let's go to the cabin."

"I'm not going to swim."

"Bobby, we swim, we sail, we canoe."

"I'm not going to swim."

It was obvious Bobby was not going to swim.

My Core Interest area is people. My Core Skills are communicating, motivating, and listening. I can help Bobby.

"How did you decide not to swim?" (**How** is far less accusatory than why.)

"Last summer, my brother drowned. My parents sent me away to boarding school. Now I'm off to camp for two months. They don't want to see me. If you think I'm going near the water, you're crazy."

Right. Bobby wasn't going to swim, and now I knew why. I agreed, and we went to the cabin to choose a bed.

I decided I had four options that could help me overcome my, and Bobby's, problem:

1. The owner of the camp was a psychiatrist, and Bobby obviously needed help. I could go to him.

2. I could go to the Waterfront Director, who had experience in teaching kids to swim.

3. I could go to my Section Director, tell him the story, and suggest he get a more experienced Counselor to work with Bobby (this was my first year as a Counselor!).

4. I could figure out how to help him myself.

My primary Core Value, as revealed by all the work I had done in the Accomplishment Section, was independence or, as I sometimes call it, control of my destiny (obviously not in a spiritual way, but as much as possible on a day-to-day basis). Others call it individuality.

So, you know which of the four options I took.

Right, number four. I'm going to work this out myself.

As I described earlier in Chapter One, on the first day, when the other kids went swimming, I took Bobby to the beach. We dug little canals up from the lake, floated sticks in them, made little pools, and put minnows in the pools and played with them. We splashed our hands in the water. Each day we followed this routine.

A few days later we got the camp dog involved. We threw sticks in the lake for the dog to retrieve. Bobby threw a stick; the dog brought it back. I threw a stick; the dog brought it back. Bobby threw another stick; the dog was bored, and didn't bring it back. I urged Bobby to go into the water to get the stick. He did, without thinking about what he was doing. The dog went after it too. They tumbled around in the water. Bobby came back with the stick, triumphantly. He had lost his fear of the water.

Soon, Bobby was swimming. He was diving. By the end of the summer, he was playing water polo. His head was pushed under water. He came up gulping, but laughing.

On the last day of camp, Bobby looked up at me as he got on the bus to go home and quietly said, "Thanks, Hurst."

If I could find a job that gives me as much satisfaction as teaching Bobby to swim, I would surely be on The Right Mountain.

Teaching Bobby to swim was a perfect match for:

1. *My core functional skills*: communicate, motivate, listen, coach, encourage

2. *My core personality skills*: independent, caring, enthusiastic, energetic, inspiring

3. *My Core Interest*: people

4. *My Core Values*: independence, making a difference

I reworked my accomplishment list to incorporate my accomplishment with Bobby, and to delete accomplishments that were not demonstrations of my Core Skills, Core Interests, and Core Values.

This section crystallizes the accomplishments that genuinely demonstrate who we are and what we have done. Go back through your accomplishments and check to see if they match up with the real you. Perhaps some of them will need to be rewritten. Perhaps some will fall by the wayside. And perhaps you'll find some new ones, as I found Bobby.

How many? Well, probably eight or ten. Enough to give breadth.

Only when you are satisfied, do you, can you, move on to the next section.

LESSONS FROM EVEREST
Things Change

In less than a minute, the sky went from blue to black. And if you are not prepared to recognize when there is such a change on the mountain, and change what you are doing, you may die.

I thought I had found all my accomplishments, but then I realized that my understanding of myself had changed and I had to go back and re-do some of it. Things change. Go with it.

Reference Point

We all use, and we all need, Reference Points in making decisions—"this is better than that. This is bigger than that; faster than…."

Review your Core Accomplishments. Which one stands out as the most relevant, most vivid, most poignant one? Which one, if you could conceptually replicate it time after time in your life, would bring you the most satisfaction? Which is equivalent to teaching Bobby to swim? Which one has the most elements that define you?

This will become your touchstone, your template, your Reference Point, upon which choices can be made confidently.

Be sure. If you can't find one that stands out from all the rest, you probably have to do some more digging, as I did to find Bobby. If you have two or three, you need to be more rigorous.

When you have found one, review it. See if you have to rewrite it to incorporate demonstrations of your Core Skills, Core Interests, and Core Values.

Get comfortable with it.

Then write it down and orally deliver it in (maximum) three minutes. We and many others call this a capsule profile. Some call it a blurb. It presents, in capsule form, the essence of you.

How does it feel?

When it starts to feel comfortable, and gives you no niggly second thoughts, then you are there. You're ready to tell the world.

You know who you are and you can prove it.

And when you reach the point where you are choosing between two or more career opportunities (and yes, that will happen!), and have to make life choices, this Reference Point will serve as a basis for that decision.

Teaching Bobby to swim is my Reference Point. It vividly demonstrates my Core Skills, Core Interests, and Core Values.

Does that mean I can only teach kids to swim? Of course not.

What it means is that I have a conceptual framework to lay across a opportunity to see if there is a match. This will become more understandable in the Job Search Section, but let me demonstrate what I mean.

If I lay "Teaching Bobby" on top of the job of a school teacher, what happens?

• It is a good match for skills, except perhaps for creativity.

• It is a good match for interests, if in fact the school is about the kids, not the curriculum or the reputation.

• It is a bad match for my Core Value of independence (you have to follow their curriculum).

How about the job of an outplacement counselor in a large firm?

• Not bad, except, perhaps, for creativity and independence.

How about a camp counselor?

• Well, money probably is going to come into my value list somewhere, because I have to support a family. And you don't find a lot of 45-year-old camp counselors.

The list goes on…

I can lay my Reference Point down on top of a job opportunity and see if there is a match. I can lay it down on top of volunteer activities, on top of decisions regarding how I spend time with my grandchildren, or on top of where I live. It is a template for everything. But you have to realize that it is a conceptual, not literal, template.

The best job and career match I found was career counseling in my own organization. Great match for my Core Skills, Core Interests, and Core Values and, in my own business, I'd be able to ensure I was working with people I'd have a successful relationship with.

Once you find, and believe in, your Reference Point, it is a fabulous tool to use as a template to test job opportunities, as well as life decisions.

It is also a great selling tool for a job. When you go in for an interview and you are at the initial or selling stage, the first question is invariably, "Tell me about yourself, who you are."

And, as you might remember, you have a maximum of three minutes to get someone's attention and interest. About 90% of the impression you make on others is made in that first three minutes. It's true of job interviews, of dates, of cocktail parties, of golf games. It is true everywhere. And, if the impression is negative, you'll have a devil of a time overcoming and changing it.

So, back to the interview. If you are applying for a job as a career counselor, the first question is liable to be: "Tell me about yourself."

If your answer is: "I'm creative, patient, a good motivator, a good listener. My real interest area is people. My Core Values are independence, and making a difference."

….you will sound like 90% of the applicants, otherwise they probably wouldn't be applying for this type of job. You have not distinguished yourself from the rest of the qualified people.

But, if you are applying for a job as a career counselor in a small firm that requires individual counselors to show creativity and be independent, and your reply to the "tell me about yourself" question is: "Let me tell you about teaching Bobby how to swim…."

And, you finish the three minutes by saying, "If you are looking for someone who has these skills, these interests, and these values, I might just be your person."

Which do you think is more revealing, more relevant, more memorable, more persuasive?

Bobby is, of course, more powerful than a string of generic adjectives.

So, a Reference Point is a great way to introduce yourself. It is a great selling tool. And for those of us with an independent streak, like me, it is a tool that helps self-select employers, because some will drop you off their list for being too independent and too creative. That's the risk you take.

But to me, to those of us who are independent, that is not a risk. In fact, it is a positive, because I don't want to work for someone who doesn't value my independence and my creativity. I won't be at my best there, so I won't be satisfied, motivated, or successful. I'll be fired or I'll quit.

The Reference Point, therefore, is a selling tool, and a self-selection tool.

Personal Allegory

There is another way of dramatically making that first three minutes work for you in both a selling and self-selective way. It is a *Personal Allegory*. An allegory is a story, a picture, or a thing in which the meaning or message is presented symbolically. And I learned about this by chance. Well, not really by chance, because in the process of discovering who you are, everything that happens is a piece of the puzzle. It is a journey.

During my searching time, before I started The Career Centre, I was volunteering everywhere I could—to watch, listen, and learn (we'll talk more about this in the Job Search Section). I volunteered and eventually became Chairman of Outward Bound Canada, during a pivotal period in my life when I discovered experiential education, learning by doing, and confirmed that I was an experiential learner. In fact, in many ways, that discovery was the basis of The Career Centre and this book. Rather than a didactic process, which uses tests to tell you who you are, this is an experiential process. We lead you through a process in which you do the work yourself; you discover who you are and really believe it.

One of my volunteer activities was the result of a phone call from a friend of mine, Eric, who ran an outplacement agency, a relocation firm. He phoned one day to ask if I'd help him out.

"Sure," I replied, "What can I do?"

"I've got eight former CEOs going through the program at our relocation firm and they have rebelled. I have to find someone to get them back on track, and I think you could do it."

"What happened?"

"Well, they've all gone through the three weeks of testing, they've gotten feedback from the shrinks, they've written their life stories, and they're about to do what we call a capsule profile."

"What is a capsule profile?"

"Well, you know the theory that you have only three minutes to make an impression in an interview. We get our clients to create a capsule profile, a three-minute statement designed to knock the socks off an interviewer.

"Today, the eight of them were sitting around a table with our consultant when one of them, Brian, the former president of Nestlé, looked across the table and said, 'Wait a minute. Wait a minute. Let me get this straight. I'm 54 years old. Three weeks ago, I was the president of Nestlé making $450,000 a year, with 1,200 employees and $750 million in sales. And now I'm sitting here and you, you're what, 34 years old? You are going to help me through this mess? I don't think so. You can't possibly understand what I'm going through. You have no idea what is going on inside me.'

"And the other seven guys agreed.

"The consultant has lost their confidence. She came to me and told me the story. It seems to me that I have a couple of options. I can put another consultant in there, an older one, or I can get someone from outside who I think could help and who they will automatically respect. Someone like you. You're a successful businessman, you've made some money, you've built a business. So, you'll walk in there and get their attention. I've known you for 30 years and I think you could help them."

I listened. I thought about it.

I like challenge. In fact, for a while, I thought challenge was my Core Value and this would certainly be a challenge. And I'm trying to learn about myself. This could be a perfect place to add to that learning.

"Sure," I said. "Let's do it. When?"

"Can you come over right now? These folks are chomping at the bit."

"What will I do?"

"I'm not sure," he said, "but I think you'll figure it out when you get in with them."

An hour later, I walked into the room. The consultant was still there. The executives were there, visibly upset because their lives and their futures were at stake, and they had lost confidence in their consultant and perhaps the process.

I introduced myself to those I didn't know, and said hi to the three that I knew; two of whom, including Brian, were once clients of my advertising agency. They were the CEOs, oops, ex-CEOs, of companies such as Black & Decker, Libby's, Liptons. All serious businesses. All accomplished people.

We got right down to business.

"What do we do now?" queried Brian.

"Well, I know you've been working on your capsule profiles, so let's start there. I want each of you to do your three-minute profile." I didn't know what else to do. I thought if they got talking, I could listen and figure it out. I remembered a phrase my business partner Chris always used before we went into a meeting: "If they're talking, we're winning."

They got up, one at a time, and did their profiles. There were eight panels on a whiteboard in the room. Taking a panel for each person, the consultant wrote down the key words that they said.

After they had finished, they were pretty pumped up. They had been saying big things about themselves. Doubling sales! Increasing profits! Introducing new brands!

They looked at me, "What do you think?"

"Fabulous. Great. I love the concept of the capsule profile. As an ex-advertising guy, it is the headline, the grabber. But what you guys have done stinks. It's useless."

There was an audible silence. They looked at me in dismay. The consultant looked at me in anger. I could hear her thinking, "We have them going. They're excited, positive. Don't put them down now."

I walked to the board and turned to them. "Brian, you're a sales guy. Mo, you're in marketing. You're an accountant, Murray. Peter, you're an engineer. I continued around the table, pointing to each of them." I listed off their professional credentials one by one.

"Now watch." I circled the words on the board that each and every one of them had used. Bottom-line oriented. Manager of change. Risk-taker. Entrepreneurial. People-skilled.

I turned to them. "Peter, you're an engineer, and you, Brian, are a sales guy. You have both listed people skills. But you don't have the *same* people skills. That's a given for an engineer and a sales-man. What you've done here is list the responsibilities of a CEO, not who you are as individuals. If I put a four-by-eight sheet of ply-wood up in front of each of you and listened to these capsule profiles, I wouldn't be able to tell one of you from the other.

"But there are huge differences. So this stuff is useless as a selling tool to differentiate yourself from the other candidates."

I sat down.

They looked at their own profiles, mumbled explanations, and finally worked themselves into agreeing with me.

"So, what are we looking for?" asked Brian. "What do we do now?"

We talked about it, and after 40 minutes had no answers.

"So, Jim," said Brian, who was becoming the spokesmen, "why don't you tell us who you are. Give us your capsule profile. Maybe that will help jump-start us."

"I've never done this before," I admitted sheepishly. "I don't have one."

"Oh, great. The blind leading the blind. Perfect."

There were sighs of resignation. After three weeks, they were nowhere.

After a few moments of deflation, Brian looked up. "Look, Jim, we've all tried it. Why don't you try it. It's five o'clock. Go home, and come back tomorrow morning at nine o'clock with your capsule profile."

The challenge was there. And I like challenge. And I was trying to figure out who I was. Perhaps this was what I needed: my peers challenging me might bring my life into focus. I might just figure out who I am.

"OK," I agreed. "I'll see you here at nine o'clock."

I drove home. We lived on a farm 45 miles from the office. At seven o'clock, I sat down in my little den and started to think.

Who am I?

At midnight, I had concluded that I was a marketing-oriented, entrepreneurial, people-skilled...the same kinds of generic words as they had used. I had nothing to show for my efforts. It was tough.

After five hours, I had nothing.

I figured I had two choices:

> One: Go to sleep, wake up, phone in, and say I don't want
>   to play anymore. After all, I wasn't getting paid.
>
> Two: Stay up all night trying to figure out who I am.

I decided to stay up all night. I had no idea what I was looking for, but I kept searching. I looked at the walls of my den, the paintings, the photos, the books. There was a theme here: the west, cowboys, horses, cattle.

Maybe I was a cowboy. Nope, he's too much of a loner. I'm independent, but I like people.

A horse? A mustang? A chuckwagon? A campfire? A fence? A pioneer? A cattle-driver? No. No. No. Nothing worked. I pressed on.

At 4:30 in the morning, I got it. I tested it a dozen times against my past accomplishments. I loved it.

I went to sleep for three hours, got up, dressed, and drove into town. On the way, I started to have second thoughts. At 4:30 in the morning, it looked great. But in the bright light of day, I was afraid I was going to embarrass myself.

I arrived at the boardroom where they had gathered the day before. I walked in. The eight were all there. The consultant was there. And they were waiting. They were looking forward to my capsule profile. They wanted to watch me squirm, as I had made them squirm.

I sat down. Another woman walked in. She looked 6 foot 18. A tall, ice-cold blonde! I got up to introduce myself.

"Good morning," she said, "I'm Doctor Tiiu Slankis. Sit down." I sat down.

"The shrink," I said to myself. "They've brought in the shrink."

"You have three minutes to tell me who you are, and you may start…." The seconds ticked by. It seemed she was waiting for the second hand to get to the top of her watch.

I swallowed. I ran my fingers under my collar. I started to panic.

"Now! Now! Start now."

I looked up.

"I'm a Wagon Master. A Wagon Master.

"Think back to the 1800s, a small town on the east coast of the U.S. Philadelphia. There are a bunch of people there. Twelve weeks ago they were in Liverpool, and they wanted to come to the new world, America, where the streets are paved in gold, where the vistas are beautiful, where the horizons go on forever.

"They hopped on a boat and sailed to America. On the way over, a third of them died, including most of the children. Finally, they got to Philadelphia. It was worse than Liverpool.

"The streets were paved in horse manure. There were no vistas, no horizons. They realized that they had made a terrible, terrible mistake.

"Then someone said, 'No, don't give up. Go west. They give out thousands of acres of free land. Go west. The vistas are beautiful, the horizons go on forever.'

"So, they decided to go west.

"But, as they were preparing, they realized that they had no experience with horses, wagons, rivers like the Mississippi, Indians, and mountains. And, because they had no experience, they had no confidence.

"So, they sat in Philadelphia, and they dreamed.

"Then one day, a wagon-train came to town. At the head of it was a Wagon Master. He had experience with horses, wagons, rivers, Indians, and mountains. And, his experience gave them the confidence to go west. To achieve their dreams.

"In business, I was a Wagon Master. I owned advertising agencies, PR firms, research firms. Eventually, I owned part of The Kettle Creek Canvas Co., Smith & Jamieson Tea, The Arctic Trading Co.

"What did I do in the advertising business? Well, I was not a good account man. I didn't do the creative. I didn't do the finances. What did I do?

"In fact, as I looked back, I realized that what I did in all my businesses was walk around and listen to people. I learned about their dreams. Bill wanted to start an independent research company, but said he had no experience with business plans, finances, accountants, lawyers. Melanie had a small business, but didn't have any experience with business disciplines, financing, strategic planning. And on and on.

"As I listened to them, I realized that I had the experience they didn't have.

"So the combination of their dreams, and my experience, resulted in them having the confidence to create or expand each of their businesses.

"In business, I was a Wagon Master."

There was dead silence. Then, the engineer spoke up. "No, Hayhurst, what you are is an *idiot*. You can't go into an interview for a president's job and say you are a *Wagon Master*."

There were murmurs of agreement.

"Wait a minute," I said. "Let's talk about this. The first thing you are trying to do with this capsule profile is distinguish yourself from everyone else, all the other applicants. I submit that tomorrow, a week from now, a year from now, you will all remember the Wagon Master. But you won't remember the bottom-line oriented, manager of change, risk-taker, entrepreneurial, people-skilled guy.

"Secondly, it's self-selective. Peter, the engineer, says I'm an idiot. In three minutes, he has decided he and I can't work together. And he's probably right. He's logical and straightforward, I'm off-the-wall. We're entirely different. We probably can't work together.

If I were a smart interviewee and just wanted a job, I could probably figure out what he wants. Then I could contort myself to be that and he'd hire me. Once on the job, I'd have two choices: stay contorted and not be very effective, and he'll fire me; or, relax and be myself, which is not what he wanted…and he'll fire me.

"So, in three minutes, we can both make a decision. A job with Peter is not the right job for me. There is no wasted time."

The group was intrigued. The Wagon Master story had their attention. They all drew pictures of me in their minds. It described who I was perfectly. They loved the concept and each of them committed to searching for a unique capsule profile, a Reference Point, and, if possible, a Personal Allegory. It was a breakthrough for them, and for me. I now knew positively who I was and could describe it in a unique, memorable way. That discovery, that insight, has changed my life. Because I now know *who I am*.

Later, I learned that the allegory technique is also job-selective. Eric, my friend who had brought me in, heard the Wagon Master story and loved it. He invited me into his office for a chat.

"How would you like to work here?" he asked. "I've heard your story. Everyone is talking about it. I think you'd be great in this business. In fact, that is really why I asked you to help out. I thought we'd both see that you'd be great."

I thought about it. I lay the Wagon Master as a template on top of the job he was offering and tried to match them.

"Nope," I said, "it's not right for me."

"Why not?" he asked. "It seems so perfect."

"Well, if you tease apart the Wagon Master, it is a perfect description of me. It pulls out and demonstrates my Core Skills, Core Interest Areas, and Core Values. In fact, it makes listing these essences of me very easy.

"I certainly have the skills to work within this business: patience, listening, creativity, motivation. It is certainly in my interest area: people. And, it does match one of my Core Values: making a difference. But, it doesn't match my need for independence, control of my destiny. You have 12 partners here. You have meetings to decide when to have meetings. You all have to agree on everything.

"Did you ever hear of a wagon-train with 12 Wagon Masters? It doesn't happen. They're self-sufficient, independent. When the wagon-train comes to a river, the Wagon Master takes input from others, but he makes the final decision. Sometimes, he'll say, 'We have to cross now. Some of us might drown. But if we wait and the spring flood comes, we'll all drown. So we're crossing. Now.' He makes that decision. You have 12 equal partners here. You reach decisions by consensus. I don't work well in that environment. It doesn't match my *Core Value*.

"So, I can't work here. Sorry. But, thank you very much. I hope I have helped. And I know you've opened my eyes to who I really am and to a career possibility. I can be a career counselor, but in a different type of organization."

And that insight was the start of my investigation that led to the creation of The Career Centre, where I could be a Wagon Master.

How do you find your allegory? For each individual, the search is unique.

All I know is that each of our clients who have found one seem to have evidence of it in their rooms, homes, offices, or hobbies. Or, they have a memory of something that has forever stuck with them.

My office was full of cowboy stuff. I have always said, "When I grow up, I'm going to be a cowboy." Somewhere in the cowboy genre was probably going to be my allegory.

I was recently working with a client who had given up on finding his Personal Allegory. As we were winding up one meeting, he made an offhand comment about how all of this self-assessment stuff was a jigsaw puzzle. He stopped and jumped out of his chair.

"That's it," he shouted, "that's me. I solve jigsaw puzzles."

He sat down, laughing. "It was there all the time. Look at my business accomplishments. I'm always putting together corporate pieces of a puzzle. That's what I love. Look around my house. I have hundreds of jigsaw puzzles. I do them all the time!"

His joy was so profound. His allegory had been there all the time, staring him in the face.

And once I found my Personal Allegory, I tested it against my Reference Point. They must be consistent, a match.

Is Bobby a match for the Wagon Master? Let's test it.

Skills: Communicate, motivate, listen, enthusiastic, caring, inspiring.
Yes in both cases.

Interests: People.
Yes in both cases.

Values: Independence, making a difference.
Yes in both cases.

The only possible difference is that it is one person, Bobby, versus a wagon-train. But in fact, I deal with the individuals in each wagon to motivate and care for them. And I have to listen to them, to their individual needs. Finally, I certainly have to inspire them when the going gets incredibly difficult (in the mountains, after Indian attacks, on the long, tedious, hot desert, or on the plains).

Yes, on a conceptual basis it is a match.

If you think allegorically, or would like to try to find an allegory, give it a go—find your Wagon Master equivalent.

As a catalyst, here are some of the allegories that our clients have found:

> The Decoder: Decoding enemy messages was crucial to the Allies' victory in WW II. I can see patterns in peoples' behavior that make their responses to situations predictable. I decode people.

> The Alpha Wolf: The leader of the pack, but still a member of the team when the primary job, getting food, has to be done.

> The Navigator: The guy that stands beside the captain, feeding him information on the winds, the competition, the morale, and the physical capability of the team.

> The Ringmaster: The ringmaster at the circus, under the big top. The organizer and promoter of others who entertain and provide laughter and happiness. I work with specialists and experts, whose work I understand but cannot do.

> The People Editor: An editor's job is to celebrate the good and savage the bad. The editor's role is to identify the problems and ask innovative and creative questions, questions that inspire the writer to think in positive

ways about the change, about the rewriting process. I do all of this, but with people, not words.

The Gardener: A gardener, with knowledge of each plant's unique requirements, tends them individually so they flourish.

The Orchestra Conductor: By themselves, each of the orchestra members plays well, but only under the leadership of a conductor can they make beautiful music.

The Alchemist: Like the alchemists of olden times who turned lead into gold, I help people turn their lives around and find bright shiny days, rather than the cloudy, dreary ones they have been enduring

Was I a Wagon Master on Everest? No. My role was a team member, responding to our leader. And I understood this after laying the Wagon Master template on top of the task confronting us. There was not a match. And so I knew I would have to modify my behavior on the climb to be an effective, contributing member of the team.

There will always be times when I can, and must, modify my behavior for a short period of time. But I have to do it consciously and be aware of my true self and the changes I need to make in order to be successful in the new environment.

The Wagon Master allegory evokes images in everyone that hears it, and they quickly know my skills, interests, and values. They also know I like the outdoors, so they start to draw pictures in their minds about me. It makes me memorable and distinctive. And that's part of what we want to do with this capsule profile.

Throughout history, we have used parables, metaphors, stories, and allegories to teach, to help people remember. So if you find an allegory (and again I point out that a large portion of the population won't), this is another very effective way to create a capsule profile. About 40% of the people who have gone through our Career Centre develop a Personal Allegory and the rest use a Rreference Point to tell their stories. Both work very effectively.

LESSONS FROM EVEREST
The Wagon Master by David Sanders

This original piece hangs in my office and is a constant reminder of my role in helping others achieve their dreams.

CHAPTER NINE

Summary of the Learnings

Now let's gather all that we have learned in one place, both to refresh our memories and to provide a one-page reference sheet. Does your life, who you are, fit on one page? Hard to imagine it will, isn't it? But let's try.

Usually people find that they can remember and effectively use, only three things at a time. Perhaps that is why history is full of threes: the three wise men, the three musketeers, three coins in a fountain, and on and on.

In the previous exercises, we have often gathered and sometimes prioritized more than three items, and that's fine. Our bet is that, in the final analysis, you'll always remember and use three. Let's see what they might be.

Take a page in your binder and make a list like this (see www.therightmountain.com):

- Core Skills

  1. Functional (three)

  2. Personality (three)

  3. Knowledge (three, if possible)

- Core Interests area

- Core Values (three)

- Relationships (three)

- Reference Point

- Personal Allegory

How does it feel?

Sometimes our clients get to this stage and say WOW!

Sometimes there is still a little niggle that there is something missing. In this case, we suggest that they live with it a while, noodling their answers. It is kind of like a detective knowing that there is one piece of the puzzle missing. They go back over all the data, massage it, and—pop—out comes the missing piece.

We've had clients at this stage all of a sudden remember another accomplishment, one that becomes a Reference Point.

Remember, *The Right Mountain* is a journey.

So, that's it. That's the experiential way to figure out who you are. You do it by looking back at *where you have gone right*. And once you find out who you are, you can apply this to personal or job decisions. You look back at where you have gone right, to figure out who you are, so that you can make better career and life decisions.

And oh, by the way, now that you know who I am, you can probably understand how I became a career counselor, and why I started my own business rather than work for someone else. And, if you look at what I do in my personal life, from making time in my office for my grandchildren, to starting a charity for kids from the inner-city rather than working for one already established, you will see a consistent pattern: I teach Bobby to swim. I'm a Wagon Master.

Now that you know who you are and can prove it, you have the template to help you recognize *The Right Mountain* for you in your career and in your life.

LESSONS FROM EVEREST

The Right Mountain is a journey, not a destination.

PART

TWO

Getting the Job and Life You Want

CHAPTER TEN

Job Search

We started this process by stating that you have to know who you are before you can make the best career and life decisions. And now that you know who you are, it's time to figure out the where and the what and the how. It is job search time.

Let's do a brief overview of this often mystifying and bewildering process.

Job Searches

Simply speaking, there are two kinds of job searches:

- Changing jobs in the same career area

- Changing careers

And, because most of us will change employers about eight times in our working life, we had better know the difference. Which one are you doing? It makes a difference because if you are simply changing jobs in the same career area, your past accomplishments will be powerful selling tools.

However, if you are looking at a career change, you will have to learn to *conceptualize* your past accomplishments to make them relevant to new areas.

Approaches

There are at least six approaches to consider in searching for a job.

1. Mailing Out Résumés to H.R. Departments

Forget it! Somewhere between 99% and 100% of these mailings will be thrown away by employers. I have not heard of anyone who got a job this way.

2. Answering Ads in Trade Journals

Small chance of success. About 90% of those trying this technique found their jobs through other means. And it only works if you are staying in the same career area. Don't count on it.

3. Answering Newspaper Ads

Most useful in lower salary or hourly wage categories. Local papers have the best success rate, but it is still 20% or less. Again, it works best if you are in the same career area.

4. Search Firms

The success rate here seems to be improving, but, it is still less than 25%. Remember, these firms are working for, and are paid by, the employers, so don't expect them to be focusing on helping you. Don't leave the search up to them. They are most effective at the more senior levels. Often relationships are built here when senior executives hire those firms to fill job openings in the companies they run. Then, when the executives get fired and start their own job search, they go back to them for help. The lesson? It is wise to treat people with respect on the way up because you may meet them on the way down. For most of us, especially in down times, this is not an effective resource.

5. The Internet

Here, you prepare a résumé, post it on one (or more) of the job-posting sites, and wait for a call that there is a match. Or, you look for matches. It is fast, simple, and works best for specific skill occupations. It works well if you are changing jobs in the same career area, and for graduating students. There are, perhaps surprisingly, some interesting geographic differences. In Canada, 12% used the Web, while only 6% in the United States found a job this way.

The list of job search sites grows almost every day, so you have to keep in touch with this area. It is useful just as a catalyst because it gives you an idea of another contact, or another interesting job, or an exciting industry.

When you look into this area, you will find sites for:

• Recent college graduates, with postings for companies, relocation tools, free e-mail, scholarship searches, career articles, and chat rooms

• Labor market information, outlooks, and workplace issues

• Job fairs and job matching services

• Opportunities around the world, from entry level to senior management positions in private, public, and voluntary sections

This resource is an enormous, ever-changing, and wonderful, if a little overwhelming, catalyst. We really encourage you to visit the Internet daily! One friend of mine has hired two aeronautical engineers for his company in North America this way. And one of them came from Bulgaria.

6. Networking/Informational Interviewing

This method has several subsections, which we'll later discuss in detail because it is without doubt the one you should focus on. Essentially, this is the technique with the highest success rate, over 42% globally, and higher in North America.

Anyone searching for a job should be aware of, and keep in touch with, all of these approaches, because you never know where an idea or a contact might come from.

What will the job search be like? Much like self-assessment, it is simple but not easy.

It will take longer than you think. *The New York Times* reports that an individual's average length of time out of work has been rising over the last two years, from 13 weeks to 18 weeks. And that is an *average*. Some support groups for the unemployed now hold separate sessions just for those who have been out of work more than six months!

You start by writing, rewriting, and fine-tuning your résumé.

Then you begin the search for jobs that match your skills, interests, and values.

Then you look for organizations that have those jobs and have your values.

Then the true job search starts, securing job interviews with decision makers.

It will be a roller-coaster ride—exciting when you see a potential great fit, disappointing when you get rejected.

The biggest challenge for all of us, as our client Maggie notes, is dealing with constant rejection. It is tough on self-esteem. You start second-guessing everything you have done, and wonder if someone has permanently turned off the light at the end of the tunnel!

Find a support group. Ad hoc groups have sprouted up in virtually every city in North America and the rest of the world. Find peers, former associates, and friends who are also job hunting, and talk regularly. Talk about schedules and research, practice mock interviews, share highs and lows. Give each other structure, something to look forward to, something to keep up motivation.

Maggie also recommends doing something outside the search where you know you can have some success. It doesn't matter what it is—a part-time job, a fitness training goal, a math course, fly tying, painting, or babysitting your grandchildren. It is essential to have something where you invest effort and see positive results. That keeps you going, otherwise the glass is not only half-empty, it is emptying fast.

Remember, it takes commitment. Do it one step at a time. Just like Everest.

Let's get started.

CHAPTER ELEVEN

Understanding
the Hiring Process

First, let's look at this from the employer's side so we understand what we are up against.

- They hate the hiring process.

  - It takes enormous time and energy.

  - It can result in accusations of discrimination or unfair hiring, thereby wasting valuable time and money.

  - It is costly.

- They would rather promote from within.

- They would rather network through current employees, friends, or colleagues.

- They want the applicant to make the decision easy for them. That means an interviewee who can *prove* that he/she has accomplishments relevant to the job being discussed. This takes the guesswork out of the hire.

- They want to make the process as painless as possible; nobody likes to say no face-to-face with an applicant. Therefore, they want to start with résumés, not face-to-face discussions.

- Interestingly, in case studies we monitored in a large multinational and a private mid-sized organization, we learned that:

  - The pile of 200 résumés was quickly culled into three groups—yes, no, and maybe—with less than 45 seconds given to each individual résumé.

  - The "Maybes" were then given another 60 seconds.

  - The final "Yes" group was given about 90 seconds to see if they really should be in that category. These accounted for less than 20% of the total reviewed.

  - In each case, individual words that proved relevant accomplishments were circled, and only those applicants with four or more circled words were granted face-to-face interviews.

  - Less than 2% of applicants received job offers. Tough competition. It means all the work you did in the self assessment is going to give you a leg up.

    Historically, companies have found that:

- 80% of applications/résumés are discarded

- 20% get a first interview

- 5% get a second interview

- 1% to 2% get a job offer

  We tried to find out why hiring organizations rejected so many applicants. The answers were revealing:

- The applicant doesn't know who he, or she, is.

- The applicant cannot describe their accomplishments.

• The applicant cannot relate their accomplishments to the job being discussed.

• The applicant does not demonstrate knowledge about, or interest in, the company, its products, or its policies.

• The applicant does not participate effectively in the interview.

It has been said that 98% of all applicants are not able to effectively present themselves in the résumé and/or interview. We also know that a large majority of hirers are bad interviewers. That makes it a tough game. But it is easier for *you* because you know who you are. In fact, everyone's job becomes easier. And it improves your chances of success, because you can answer questions the interviewer doesn't even know he or she should ask!

You can help the interviewer by demonstrating that:

• You know who you are.

• You know what your accomplishments are.

• You know **how** your accomplishments are relevant to the job being discussed.

Before we discuss the process, résumés, and interviews, here are a couple of thoughts about the hiring organizations' methodology.

Assuming the relevant skills/knowledge are present in all the final candidates, companies then judge applicants on their:

Initiative	Judgment	Leadership
Enthusiasm	Adaptability/Versatility	Decision-Making
Problem Solving	Communication Skills	

Companies, because they believe the past—*where you have gone right*—is a good predictor of the future, judge these attributes based on relevant accomplishments in:

Work Experiences

Extracurricular & Volunteer Activities

Marks and Professor's Comments
(in the case of recent graduates)

In the final analysis, companies are looking for interviewers to talk:

ACCOMPLISHMENTS, NOT RESPONSIBILITIES

They want to know what you did do with your responsibilities—how you added value—not just that you could do the job required!

Now let's look at it from your perspective. You have all this information. You've got a leg up!

But even when you do a great job in the interview, and are a perfect fit for the job, it is still not easy. Things don't happen fast enough for you. Why? Because the hirer has other things, and other people, on her mind. You probably won't get invited back or offered the job the next day, or even the next week. This is a huge priority for you, but not necessarily for her.

• Be patient, keep in touch, e-mail interesting and relevant articles to her. That keeps you top of mind.

• Forget a sense of entitlement—no one owes you a job.

• Job searching is a job. Work at it 9 to 5, or longer. In fact, many interviews will be at the end of the day or over an early morning breakfast.

• Persistence, patience, and flexibility are critical.

• Find a support group. This is tough work.

- It is a numbers game. One job searcher told me that he talked to 136 people in a six-week period—that's an average of over four per day! But, he received four job offers! You have to be the right person in the right place at the right time.

- The majority of the jobs are in organizations with less than 50 people. These organizations are harder to find, as they are less well-known. They also hardly ever have H.R. departments. That is both good and bad news. The bad is that the people you meet will not be trained interviewers. The good is that, if you are well prepared, you can help them make positive decisions quickly.

- You never get a second chance to make a first impression. Everyone, everywhere, during the search, or at a party, a ball-game, or a chance meeting on the street, is a potential reference.

- Don't, don't, don't start networking or even talking to friends about your search until you are absolutely sure you can articulate, clearly, and concisely, who you are. The Self-Assessment Section focused on this, but let's be sure that you can articulate who you are clearly, and can prove it confidently.

- Write, rewrite, and rewrite again your Reference Point and/or Personal Allegory until it is second nature to you. Practice it out loud in front of a mirror and then, and only then, on close friends, spouses, or relatives. And only listen to their feedback on execution, not content. Don't let them tell you who you are, but do let them tell you about your language, your posture, your speed of delivery, and then make changes if you agree.

Now, before you begin your actual job search, you need to build an effective résumé.

CHAPTER TWELVE

The Résumé

Every single résumé must be accomplishment-based. Never, never use responsibilities. Employers only want to know what you did with your responsibilities, how you added value to the organization.

We are often asked about the best résumé style, meaning chronological or functional. There is no simple answer to this, except to say that most employers, and certainly the smaller organizations who do most of the hiring these days, are more comfortable with the chronological style. The functional style résumé is in essence, skill-based. Hirers are not used to this style, so perhaps we should make it simple for them. But it is your choice.

Remember the case studies we talked about earlier? In the first run-through of résumés, each got less than 45 seconds!

Keep your résumé short and simple. Unless you are going for an academic job, where they want to know everything (and seem to have the time to review it), we'd love to see all résumés kept to **ONE PAGE**! Impossible? Most of the top MBA programs insist on one page for their graduates' résumés, even if you are 45 years old and have had a number of successful careers before going back to school.

Someone, I'm not sure who, once said:

"I would have written you a shorter letter,
but I didn't have time."

It is so true. It takes time.

Not convinced that shorter is better? Here are the comments of a senior human resources manager on a one-page résumé presented to a major corporation by one of our clients:

"What initially caught my attention was the fact that the résumé was only one page. As an interviewer, this by itself was enough to get my attention. I don't have the time, and sometimes the patience, for two-, three-page, or longer autobiographies.

"Using the allegory made it unique and interesting and whetted my appetite for more, because it was relevant to our needs.

"I liked the accomplishments, and the facts backed them up. I liked the use of everyday language, i.e., the way people really speak! It established a personality; it was like looking at a photograph.

"Ultimately it made it easy for me to decide yes or no. And I said yes."

In the Self-Assessment Section, we listed a number of Core Accomplishments. We are going to use them now.

Some of you might remember in grade eight when we had to do our first précis. Well, we are going to do it again. Précis each of your accomplishments down to a maximum of six lines. You can use bullet points if you like. Remember the principle in writing accomplishments from the first section of this book: use the Problem/Action/Result format—PAR.

Writing the résumé has two purposes:

1. It helps you find the words you want to use to describe your accomplishments; therefore, you will be more comfortable using them in an interview.

2. It demonstrates, through accomplishments, your skills, interests, and values to a prospective employer.

Before your final edits, check for the following:

- Are you using a Reference Point or Personal Allegory at the top of the page? If not, how are you distinguishing yourself?

- Do you have at least five Core Accomplishments, all of which consistently demonstrate your Core Skills, Core Interests, and Core Values?

- Have you massaged the words, looking for action and unusual words that will grab their attention?

- Is your capsule profile concise, descriptive, and intriguing?

- Is the résumé truly yours? Could anyone else put their name on it? Is it enduring, memorable?

For years I went to business schools to recruit. I would meet 10 to 12 students a day, one day after another, for three days. When I left, I would put all the résumés in a box and put it in the corner of my office. Five days later, I would set aside an hour to try to remember individuals whom I had interviewed. Usually three or four stuck out in my mind, primarily because of a dramatic, relevant accomplishment. I would look for those résumés and, if they corresponded to my recall of the individual, he/she would be invited in for an interview. Even from the top schools, only one or two would be invited for a second interview. Most students weren't prepared for the rigor of the résumé, or the interviewing process.

We are often asked if there are verbs or adjectives that are more effective than others in catching interviewer's attention. We would obviously prefer that you find your own, that they grow out of your accomplishments. But we do understand the request and recognize that a list can be a catalyst.

Here is a list of result-oriented verbs that, where appropriate and relevant, attract attention.

RESULTS-ORIENTED VERBS

Accelerated		Devised		Launched	
Accomplished		Directed		Led	
Advanced		Edited		Maximized	
Arbitrated		Eliminated		Motivated	
Assessed		Enforced		Negotiated	
Assimilated		Engaged		Organized	
Attained		Enhanced		Owned	
Built		Excelled		Presented	
Captured		Executed		Satisfied	
Chaired		Extended		Secured	
Coached		Focused		Sold	
Conceived		Founded		Solved	
Concentrated		Generated		Stimulated	
Controlled		Headed		Streamlined	
Convened		Implemented		Strengthened	
Converted		Improved		Succeeded	
Convinced		Increased		Thrived	
Created		Influenced		Unified	
Decided		Initiated			
Defined		Innovated			
Delegated		Inspired			

This is a list of results-oriented adjectives that can be used, where appropriate and relevant, in your résumé.

RESULTS-ORIENTED ADJECTIVES

Appealing		Exhaustive		Intricate	
Competitive		Explicit		Intriguing	
Comprehensive		Extensive		Motivated	
Credible		Fulfilled		Novel	
Distinctive		Guaranteed		Opportune	
Enduring		Illustrious		Perceptive	
Energetic		Impressive		Stimulating	
Enlightened		Ingenious		Strategic	
Enterprising		Innovative		Substantial	
Enthusiastic		Instructive		Ultimate	
Essential		Integral		Unique	
Exceptional		Intelligent		Valued	
Exclusive		Intensive		Vibrant	

Wordsmith your accomplishments. Write, rewrite. Make them tight and make them action-oriented.

Do the same for your Reference Point or your Personal Allegory, whichever one you are going to use as your capsule profile (in six lines) at the top of your résumé.

Which one? It depends on you and your comfort level. If you are prepared to be totally self-selective, we like the Personal Allegory because the reaction to it will give you a sense of the mind-set of the prospective employer.

Here are some examples of Reference Points. We believe these should go at the very top of résumés to introduce you to the reader. Analyze them, critique them. See if you can pull out the skills, interests, and values. If you can, great. If not, then make sure yours is better. These are not set out as examples of perfection, but simply as catalysts to get you thinking. These are generally called, as we said earlier, capsule profiles.

Reference Points

With very little practical hockey knowledge or experience working with kids, or in a team environment, I accepted a voluntary position as a manager of a friend's hockey team. Despite these initial limitations I quickly earned the trust and confidence of the parents, players, and coaches. I have become an integral part of the team where my opinion is respected and sought after by all parties.

I once started a course in children's fiction by sitting cross-legged in front of them and reading the class a story. The students were mostly teachers and children's librarians and a lot of them had taken similar courses before. Almost without exception they told me that my course had made them think in different ways and see their roles in a different light.

By creating custom reports that had never existed before, I was able to satisfy my manager's appetite for specific, on-the-spot financial information. My efforts were highlighted when the director of finance asked me to stay on for six months after the sale of the company to help in the wind-down of operations.

By demonstrating my ability to relate to various levels of management, I earned the position of liaison between campaign staff and the sales force. My success as a troubleshooter was noted by an influential director, who instructed the personnel department to hire me on a full-time basis when my contract was completed.

I doubled the number of sailing participants from the previous year by creating a racing program, restructuring classes, and tapping the experience of my instructors.

I opened an innovative toy store that, for the first time, made playthings accessible to children in a totally touchable environment. When this unique philosophy found acceptance, I opened a second store.

Realizing that our computer could help us work more effectively by tracking client information, and more efficiently by freeing up additional time to service clients, I initiated a customized progress database and accounting system that improved productivity 20%.

Personal Allegories

This is an alternative that can go at the top of your résumé. The most effective set-up seems to be to have the allegory in the first paragraph, and then the relevant accomplishments in the second paragraph. Are the skills, interests, and values obvious and consistent?

The Settler

The Pilgrims courageously left England in the 17th century for a journey across the ocean to a foreign land. Their predecessors, know as "settlers," helped them adapt to a whole new environment and to deal with fundamental changes in lifestyle. With their collective support the Pilgrims overcame many obstacles to establish the colonial settlement of Plymouth.

Whether assisting the blind, helping a client adjust to group home living, encouraging a chronically ill woman to draw, or interacting with people on my travels, I have been a settler.

The Woodcarver

Woodcarving is an analytical process. Before beginning, the carver views the wood from all sides, carefully considering the knots and the direction of the grain to recognize the essence of the form he can release from within the wood. Working in partnership with the wood, the carver systematically develops the envisioned shape, bringing life to the wood.

I, too, have been a woodcarver, using my ability to analyze, envision, and communicate with other people and organizations to help them develop to their fullest potential.

The Setter

In the game of volleyball the pivotal player is the setter. It is the setter's job to anticipate what is needed and align the team on a plan. This player is a catalyst for the team to consistently achieve their best performance. A setter's ability to communicate openly, and to keep trying new plays, enhances the results.

From setting up group processes in the trade marketing department, and facilitating group problem-solving in the sales department, to designing impactful learning environments for managers and students, I have been a setter.

Résumé Thought-Starters

Due to the confidential nature of résumés, we will not reprint them in their entirety. However, as a catalyst, we have included my own college graduation résumé and my résumé 30 years later (which *doesn't* legibly fit on one page of this book, but does fit onto one regular 8.5 X 11 inch paper!), and some examples of accomplishment statements from résumés. We have also included statements from résumés as we first saw them (Before), and the revisions that were done upon completion of our programs (After).

There are all kinds of set-ups for résumés, but the most well-recognized style includes:

• Name, address at top

• Capsule profile, either as an allegory or Reference Point, next. Historically people have often put a list of adjectives or skills here. Our feeling is that these will always be too generic, so we don't encourage it

• Relevant accomplishments in chronological order, starting with the most recent

• Academic credentials (if you are a recent graduate, this might go under your Reference Point or allegory)

• Interests are often throwaways, but if you have a unique and/or unusual interest, and it is relevant (see my second résumé and the reference to my life as a cowboy), it can be included here

• References are often included. Generally we don't think these should be on a résumé, because we like to tailor them to the specific job.

Whether or not you put References on your résumé, here are some general guidelines worth rembering.

• References should be readily available and should be aware that they may be called on

• If an employer wants to check your references, remember that the responses your reference gives to specific questions can affect the decision to hire or not to hire you. So choose your references carefully! Tell them about the job you are seeking and remind them of your relevant experience.

Most employers check references to confirm:

• Academic qualifications

• Work and extra-curricular activities

• Strength and role in accomplishments

• Ability to work with others

• Stability, reliability

• Weaknesses

In other words, the qualities they look for in the interviews are the qualities they will attempt to confirm with your references. If you have not had recent contact with your references, drop by and bring them up to date. Not only will they be better references, but they may have some other contacts or job ideas for you.

Oh, please be sure to ask all references for their approval before you give out their names.

Jim's College Résumé

James F. P. Hayhurst

255 Sydenham Street   109 Dunvegan Road
London, Ontario N6A 1W4   Toronto, Ontario M4V 2P9

"Marketing Manager of The U.C. Ball during the year that turned
it from a consistent money loser into a $15,000 profit maker."

1959-1963   University of Western Ontario
School of Business Administration

In addition to the business courses, I am enrolled in a Masters Sociology Course in recognition of my belief that people, relationships, and communication are vital to long-term business success. I was elected Treasurer of my fraternity, and Inter-Faculty Football All-Star. I am the top salesman for the student newspaper and I successfully raced an MGB at Harewood.

As Marketing Manager of The U.C. Ball:

1) I undertook an analysis of previous years' dances:
   - they attracted senior students only, utilized small local bands, and lost money consistently

2) I undertook research to determine attitudes about the dance

3) I recommended, got agreement to, and implemented:
   - the hiring of a big-name band (Les Brown)
   - the marketing of the dance to seniors, juniors, and sophomores (the latter two did not have their own dance)
   - a ticket price increase

Results: A profit of $15,000; an 80% attendance increase

1954-1959   Upper Canada College
Senior Matriculation

Summer Experience

1962   Taylor Statten Camps: CIT Section Director
Created a cohesive team of forty eight 18-year-old boys by challenging other staff groups to games, writing a CIT song, and leading them in a "team-building" prank.

1960   Taylor Statten Camps: Counselor
Perhaps my most significant accomplishment was cajoling a 12-year-old camper with a morbid fear of the water (his brother had drowned) to return to the water—swim, and play water polo—and enjoy it.

Jim's Current Résumé

James F. P. Hayhurst

378 Fairlawn Ave., Toronto, ON Canada • M5M 1T8 • 416-785-7700 • jim@therightmountain.com

THE WAGON MASTER

In the 19th century, people dreamed of a new life in the American West. But they didn't have the confidence to make the trek themselves, due to their lack of experience with challenges such as Indians and mountains. So they hooked up with a Wagon Master, an individual whose experience with these challenges gave them the confidence to pursue their dreams.

While building more than a dozen successful businesses, revitalizing Outward Bound Canada, counseling emerging-growth companies, creating and building a successful Career Centre, and co-creating and building a unique youth charity, I have been a Wagon Master.

CO-CREATOR AND CHAIRMAN, **Trails Youth Initiatives**   1992–present
Recognizing that prevention was a vital gap in programs for inner-city youth, I co-created and am Founding Chairman of a unique and highly acclaimed youth program. Last year 76% of our graduates went on to college!

CREATOR AND FOUNDER, **The Right Mountain Inc.**   1988–present
Realizing that our experiences as members of the 1988 Canadian Mount Everest climb were metaphors for success in professional and personal life, I created an inspirational speech, corporate workshops, and a highly acclaimed book. The speech has inspired corporations and individuals around the world. The book is in its eighth printing.

CREATOR AND FOUNDER, **The Hayhurst Career Centre**   1987–present
Recognizing a growing dissatisfaction with traditional career counseling, I analyzed the systems used and then created a unique program that has helped over 500 individuals squeeze more satisfaction out of their careers and their personal lives.

CHAIRMAN, **Outward Bound Canada**   1986–1987
I was the catalyst that caused the two Schools in Canada, which had operated independently for over 10 years, to meet and find bonds on which to build a long-term relationship.

CHAIRMAN, **Hedwyn Communications**   1982–1986
I provided the stimulus that took Hedwyn, an advertising holding company, outside its traditional fields into financial and personal growth investments in The Kettle Creek Canvas Company, The Arctic Trading Company, and the Smith & Jamieson Tea Company.

The Hayhurst Group of Companies   1966–1986

After being an employee for six years, I purchased a $20 million advertising agency, ranked 22nd in the industry, and built a group of eight companies billing over $140 million, ranking in the top three. Between 1982 and 1985, I completed arrangements with agencies in 28 countries to form a world-wide association and a base for equity control.

Procter & Gamble Canada Limited   1963–1966

University of Western Ontario, School of Business Administration, HBA   1959–1963

In fourth year, I recorded straight As, was chosen Merit Award winner, was offered a Fellowship in Sociology, and was an Inter-Faculty Football All-Star.

INTERESTS   My family, my friends, and my other life…as a cowboy.

Accomplishment Statements

Most of us like to be shown examples as a trigger to get our minds going. So here are some accomplishment statements as thought-starters. We are not suggesting they are perfect or even, in some cases, grammatically correct, but they may be a catalyst for you.

Associate, Investor Services Division

- Performed extensive cash flow and asset analysis of four emerging Israeli growth companies (revenues up to $10 million), whose respective managements had no experience in corporate valuation.

- Advised management on alternative methods of raising capital, and developed business plans on their behalf as a means of securing foreign equity capital. Three of the four firms met with investors prior to my departure.

• Designed and built client-specific computer models for three firms requiring more sophisticated methods of analyzing new ventures. All three had been implemented on my departure.

Coordinator, Film & Drama Programming

• Produced a prime-time anthology series, *Short stories*, which was expanded from one to two hours weekly under my direction as a result of its ratings and financial success.

• Initiated A&E's first foreign short film co-production venture.

Customer Service Representative

Understanding the needs of customers and management, I consistently exceeded my call quota by 33%, regularly filled vacancies in other departments, and completed special projects that improved company procedures. My concern for the needs of others was formally recognized at every quarterly meeting.

Temporary Placements

As a specialist handling financial clients, I continuously adapted to changing environments and the individual requests of my co-workers. My earnest and professional manner prompted two clients to offer me full-time employment in their head offices.

Instructor

As an instructor in sailing and ropes courses, I empathized with the fear and uncertainty a boy feels when his boat tips over, or when he is clinging to a rope 40 feet above the ground. I inspired more than 100 young men with the confidence and courage to cross an aerial ropes course they first perceived as impossible.

General Manager/Director

My focus on developing the potential in clients, employees, and artists while emphasizing continual improvement in the organization elevated the company to a respected leadership role within a competitive industry. Sales grew from $400,000 to $1.5 million in five years, to compete for top ranking in the market.

Realizing that a computer could help us work more effectively by tracking client information, thus freeing up time to serve our clients, I initiated a customized progress database and accounting system, which improved productivity 20%.

By providing guidance and art direction, I helped artists focus their efforts to achieve personal goals. One photographer, who had initially decided to quit due to lack of funds, multiplied his earnings five times in a five-year period.

International Franchise Liaison

Traveling overseas, I helped new licensees create their businesses from scratch. As coach and mentor, I supported three licensees in developing successful businesses in Stockholm, Oslo, and Tel Aviv, while remaining sensitive to their cultures and local market conditions.

Operations Manager

I instilled the company's overall philosophy and goals in my staff of 12 by hiring people who had an intrinsic interest in our business. As a result, employees initiated new ideas, and worked without an interim manager when I had to travel two weeks out of every five.

Seeing the potential of a new and growing business, I created marketing programs and operational systems that facilitated the 400% sales growth of the company. These systems were adopted by corporate headquarters as models for future franchises.

Account Executive

Art directors and designers called me to help them develop their creative strategies so they could hone in on their specific photographic needs. We then supplied the images to complete their ads. As a preferred supplier, I billed over $300,000 in sales, the second highest in the company.

Publicist

The year before I joined the company, not one artist was interviewed by the media as a result of publicity efforts. Since I joined, I have secured three magazine, 11 newspaper, nine radio, and one television appearance. Rather than continue a system of regular press releases, which were ineffective in capturing the media's attention, I chose specific events worthy of publicity, determined my media targets, designed promotional packages, and telephoned the media before and after the event.

Booking Agent

When an employee left, I was given two weeks of preparation time to replace him as manager/booking agent for three artists. I had no prior experience. My immediate priority was to find and book 10 engagements in order to secure a touring grant. Having no knowledge of sponsors, I went through old files to find venues where the artists had toured. I phoned these past sponsors, explained my situation, and by encouraging them to find new sponsors I was able to confirm 10 bookings and save the grant.

My second task was to book my artists in two states where they had never toured. I attended a conference in New York and followed up with each delegate. These delegates alone did not provide enough sponsorship to sustain a tour. With no market resources at my disposal I decided to approach the school market. I phoned telephone operators, got details on the local school systems, and, with that knowledge, was able to secure a tour.

Alumni Association Member

My ability to gain the trust and confidence of the directors has allowed me to restructure and reorganize the Board. I have had their full support in creating new officers, and in appointing new directors to fill these and other vacant positions. The Board now services its two constituencies, the undergraduate members and alumni, more responsibly and effectively.

Account Supervisor

My clients' high level of satisfaction resulted in my promotion twice within one year. The assets under my administration increased from an initial level of $100 million to nearly $6 billion. This reflected my rigorously learning the needs and wants of my clients, the intricacies of the company's computer systems, the regulations governing securities settlement, and the custodial business, and my dedication to a high level of client service. I also took the initiative to help develop better methods (i.e., computer programs) for serving clients.

Before and After Statements

The following are included to show how you can take the *responsibility* statements we found in résumés (Before) and make them into *accomplishment* statements that hirers demand (After). This work will have been done in the Self-Assessment section of this book, but hopefully these examples will crystallize the differences and stimulate you.

Candidate A

Before **Body Tech Director**

Responsible for starting up the fitness testing department for the fitness center. Management duties included developing and designing a version of the test protocol, hiring and training employees, scheduling, and overseeing the center.

After **Body Tech Director**

I set up, purchased equipment, and hired and trained a staff of 10 for the newest and largest health and fitness center. I recognized the need for an adaptation to the parent company's fitness evaluation, and designed a program analysis form. Acceptance of my recommendations by management, and constant thanks from members, were indications of my success.

Before **Canoe Trip Counselor**

Planned and led a one-month canoe trip for six 14- and 15-year-old girls. My goals included getting to know my campers, and having a safe and fun experience in the wilderness.

After **Canoe Trip Counselor**

I planned, organized, and purchased the equipment for a 36-day canoe trip. I continually encouraged, motivated, and persuaded campers to overcome difficulties and to enjoy the adventure. The trip was so successful that four of the six kids and all of the staff signed up for a 52-day trip the following summer.

Before **Head of Windsurfing**

This season I had enough confidence in some of my staff that I was able to place certain individuals in charge of their own groups. I was also able to follow through with some suggestions for improvements in the program and design a manual for the future head of windsurfing.

After **Head of Windsurfing**

I set up and implemented a windsurfing instructional program, and designed criteria for five consecutive award levels. Being able to present approximately 90% of the 350 campers with handmade badges at the end of each session was especially rewarding.

Candidate B

Before **Account Representative**

Design and Communications (PA, PR, Marketing & Design)
- Research and continually build prospective client list for cold calling
- Visit and establish client's needs, business objectives, and target groups
- Build a quote on creative requirements and close the deal
- Follow the project through design, writing, art direction, print, and delivery
- Nurture a proactive relationship to produce further work: PA, PR & Marketing
- Complete projects on time and on budget with consistency and high quality
- Reason for leaving: mutual decision to move

After   **Account Representative**

Beginning without established accounts, I developed a prospective client list by placing 150 cold calls a week.

I used my persuasion skills to establish five to six appointments a week with directors of marketing, product managers, and advertising managers.

My enthusiastic selling style and my attention to detail, overcame the antagonism between the creative and sales departments.

By judging the clients' needs, I quoted more than $200,000 worth of business.

Before **Project Manager**

Production Assistant
- Long hours and deadlines under pressure
- Versatility in all production facets of film and TV commercials
- Tour operator
- Motivate tour group of 34 students and professors
- Maintain travel budget and schedule
- Organize activities, meals, transportation, and accommodations
- Political nomination meeting
- Fundraising
- Membership development
- Campaign strategies

After   **Project Manager**

Took the initiative to start my own company and sell my organization skills.

Was versatile enough to work on three different projects:

Tour Operator: Responsible for all activities outside of classroom instruction, for group of 35 students and four professors on language courses in France. Was invited to renew my contract.

Production Assistant: Demonstrated my versatility in the production of a music video and television commercials. My adaptability was rewarded with extra work.

Campaign Manager: As a paid organizer, my responsibilities included building membership, planning strategy, and execution. The candidate won and I was offered a second contract.

Candidate C

Before **Economist**

- Monitored economic conditions in Canada and the U.S., and major developments worldwide

- Assisted in the preparation of national economic forecasts for use by CMB Crowns

- Analyzed the impact of exchange rate movements on the Crown sector. Organized seminars on the economic outlook and topical economic issues

Management Services Officer

Acted as an internal consultant undertaking/coordinating projects involving policy, administrative, operations, and economic issues. Examples:

- Assessed the desirability of incorporating fiscal incentives into the local economic development strategy

- Demonstrated the feasibility of implementing a 9-1-1 emergency telephone system

- Coordinated a project that optimized the city's allocations of fire suppression resources

- Undertook a periodic review of the local economy

- Coordinated a review of the city's business assessment/ licensing system

After **Economist**

- Developed a model that projected the Crown sector would incur a $1 million net loss per year for each one-cent decline in the U.S. value of the Canadian dollar

- Evaluated the merits of the value-added tax (VAT) and a national retail sales tax relative to the existing manufacturers' sales tax, and determined that the VAT is superior in all respects with the exception of its administration and compliance costs

Management Services Officer

Operations Analysis

- Carried out a feasibility study that made possible the cost-effective implementation of 9-1-1 service

- Coordinated the Fire Station Location Study, which recommended changes to the fire department's plans for new stations, changes that would double their impact on the level of fire protection while increasing their costs just 16%

Policy Analysis

- Coordinated an interdepartmental review of the city's business assessment and licensing systems, which led to the complete revision of license fees in 1984 and to the adjustments of assessment rates to reduce inequities in 1986

- Assessed the merits of introducing fiscal incentives into the city's economic development strategy and successfully argued against their introduction

Candidate D

Before **Liquor Outlet**

Duties: Inventory, communication, promotion, stocking

After **Liquor Outlet**

Inventory Supervisor

The store that hired me had been consistently losing money for a long period of time. I was able to recognize the problem as an out-of-date and confusing inventory system.

I reorganized the inventory to relocate all the high-selling products in one area and widen the aisles in order to allow easier access to the inventory.

The reorganization facilitated the movement of liquor from the storage room to the shelves. Within two weeks, sales had increased 20%.

Before **National Park**

> Duties: Revenue collector, communication, promotion, and administration

After **National Park**

Park Attendant

> It quickly became apparent that there were no organized activities for the many children who visited the park each year.

> After negotiating time from my supervisor, I was able to initiate and develop many organized activities such as soccer, baseball, and nature hikes.

> These activities formed the cornerstone of what today is a highly developed program for kids on Beausoleil Island.

Final Points on Résumés

People often think of using colored paper to help the résumé stand out. We've seen résumés in wine bottles (vintage Peter), birch-bark canoes (applying for a job at Outward Bound), and with a ribbon around it (a present for you).

Our advice? If it is not relevant, don't do it. Typically, gimmicks cover up a lack of content.

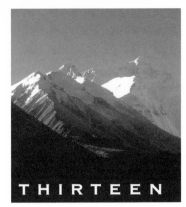

Networking

The proof is there. You would be smart to do all forms of job search, but networking appears to be the most effective. And it is simple in concept, but perhaps difficult in execution.

Start making a list of people you know. What do they do? Where do they work? Include personal friends, parents' friends, and relatives and their friends. Prioritize this list in terms of your estimate of their interest in helping you. Prioritize the list again in terms of your interest in them as people. Don't spend hours on the prioritization. We're just trying to get a starting point. (These lists should obviously be in a binder of some sort, so you can keep track of them.)

Beside the names, put titles, organizations, products, services, profitability, expansion plans, addresses, phone numbers, fax numbers, e-mail addresses, and your relationships. You have the start of your network.

We once had a client who said she didn't have a network because she had recently moved from a small town on the east coast and didn't know a soul. We asked where she was living. She shared a small apartment with two people. Ah, so she knew at least two people.

It also turned out she was doing temp work at a large publishing company. All her self-assessment accomplishments pointed towards selling. We asked if the company had salespeople. The answer was yes, but she didn't know them. Did anybody know them? Sure, in fact, one of the people at a desk near her worked for a salesperson.

Aha! Instant network. That salesperson eventually introduced her to a friend at Procter & Gamble and she got a job in sales there.

There are two keys to working with your network:

1. **Don't abuse your network or waste people's time.**

   People are usually willing to help, especially nowadays when many of us have used networks in our own job searches. But, they must believe *you* are doing at least your share, that they're not doing all the work, and that you know what you are doing. They are not in the placement business, and they don't want to offend their friends and associates by wasting their time, so you must approach them with confidence, with a specific goal, and with a plan of action.

   Start with those at the top of your priority list, those who you will be most comfortable with, those who you can be yourself with. But remember, even these people will be evaluating you, so don't meet them until you are ready.

2. **Keep expanding it.**

   Everyone you know, everyone you meet, knows others. But don't just ask for names. Once you have articulated who you are to a friend or an associate, ask if there is anyone they think would benefit from, or enjoy, meeting you. Phrase this in a way that is not "I just want to meet anyone," but rather in a way that suggests that you recognize that we all connect better with some people than others, and ask if they can think of any of their friends or associates that there could be a good match with.

We are often asked about the differences in big versus small companies and which is better. Other than the fact that small companies are doing more hiring than big companies these days, the key differences seem to be:

Big Company

- The hiring process is more standardized.

- The training program is specific.

- There is a definite structure and hierarchy.

- The salary is usually bigger.

- The work experience is specific.

- The structure provides and demands discipline.

- There is margin for learning time.

Small Company

- Hiring is done more on chemistry.

- You have immediate access to top-level people.

- There is no formal training—it is on-the-job.

- The starting salary is lower.

- The work experience is fast and broad.

- You must start producing quickly.

- There is job, personal, and compensation flexibility.

Here is a suggested contact sheet to keep track of your network (see www.therightmountain.com).

CONTACT SHEET

Company Name: _____

Contact Name/Title: _____

Address: _____

Phone/Fax/E-mail: _____

Referred to by: (name) _____

     (address) _____

     (phone/fax/e-mail) _____

Company Information (products, financial history, image, etc).

_____

_____

_____

_____

Interview Date, Time: _____

_____

Follow-up

Thank You (copy attached): _____

Résumé Sent: _____

Telephone Call: _____

Next Steps: _____

CHAPTER FOURTEEN

Informational Interviewing

W hat do you say when you call and ask for a meeting? Well, after years of testing techniques, the generally accepted practice is called "informational interviewing." You ask for an informational interview and you specifically say you are not asking for a job interview.

If you phone a friend, or a friend's friend, and say you are looking for a job, the answer will probably be, "We're not hiring." Or, if they are hiring, the answer will be, "Send us your résumé."

In many cases, even when we know who we are, we still don't know exactly what we want to do, let alone where we want to do it. So we do informational interviews in order to see what jobs are out there, and what the required skills, interests, and values are so that we can compare the hirers' needs with our assets.

The effective process is:

1. Select a name, note the connection you have with the individual, and then gather as much background as you can (likes, family, history, connections, etc.).

2. Gather as much information as you can on the organization that he/she works for (products, services, profitability, size, history, etc.).

3. Phone. You may have to do this three or four times to make contact.

4. Introduce yourself and your connection, for example:

   • My father, Don Young, suggested I call.

   • We met last week at the football game.

   • John Carroll, who works at Apex, said you would be a very interesting person to talk to. Did he call you to introduce me?

5. Say specifically that you are not looking for a job, but that you have just finished a self-assessment process and want to talk to people about the kinds of jobs and organizations that are out there.

6. Set a specific time, date, and location, and ask for less than half an hour.

7. Arrive early. Be suitably dressed. You can even ask what is appropriate attire. It indicates respect and preparation.

8. Start the informational interview.

The Informational Interview

You are going to be nervous, but that is expected. The good news is that as a result of this process you will be prepared. Here is a suggested agenda:

• Thank them for meeting with you.

• Ask his/her time availability. That lets them know you recognize the value of their time.

- Remind them up front that this is just for information. If they know they don't have to give a yes or no at the end of the session, they will be more comfortable and more talkative.

- Take notes. It is very frustrating to "tell all you know" when the person you're telling it to is not taking notes and, as a result, will most likely not remember many of your pearls of wisdom.

- Most people like to talk about themselves and what they do, so conversation should be easy if you ask good questions.

- Suggested questions:

  How did you get your job?

  What specifically attracted you to this organization?

  Would you make the same career choice? Why?

  What knowledge and skills are necessary?

  What other experiences were helpful to you in getting and doing your job?

  Are there related fields that should be explored?

  What are your Core Skills and how do you use them here?

  What values attracted you to this company?

  How does your major competition differ from you?

- After you have gathered the information, you have two choices:

  1. Thank the individual and say that when you compare your skills, interests, and values with his responses, there does not seem to be a good match. Explain why, if it seems appropriate, by using your capsule profile. That will ensure that you are remembered.

2. If there seems to be a match between you and their needs, then summarize your skills, interests, and values, either specifically or with a Reference Point or allegory. Now…pause.

   If he picks it up and says that he'd like to see you again or have you meet other people, or asks for your résumé (tell him you'll send one along; you want to be sure it is tailored to what you've learned), then whoopee!

   If he says nothing, then thank him for his time. Ask if he knows of any organizations like his that he respects, ask for individual names or perhaps even an introduction.

   In either case, be conscious of the time and be out of there on time (unless he insists on you staying).

Send a thank-you note within 24 hours. This could be by e-mail, but everyone is overloaded with e-mail so we suggest you mail it, or better still, drop it off. The note should include:

- Thank him for his time.

- Reiterate the key learnings from his comments.

The next paragraph should be one or more of the following:

- Say there is no match and that is part of what you wanted to learn.

- Point out the matches, and suggest if there ever is a need for someone like you, would he please get in touch.

- Indicate your next steps ("I've set up an appointment with Beth Henderson, as you kindly suggested. I have five meetings tomorrow, so I am certainly learning from this process.").

- Promise to keep in touch.

Never, ever, ever break the trust of informational interviewing. Never turn it into a job interview. If the employer does, fine, but don't you do it. Not only will it say something about your integrity, but it will also ruin the opportunity for future informational interviews by anyone else.

And then you repeat the process, again and again.

The key is not only the quality, but also the quantity. It is a numbers game.

The most comparable numbers game is probably selling life insurance. I had a chance to work with a group called The Top of the Table, the top 200 insurance salesmen in the world. I took the opportunity to talk to the number one agent in the world and I asked him how he did it. For five years in a row he had been number one in the world. How did he ever meet enough people, new people, year after year, to achieve these results?

He asked me if I had been an athlete. I said yes, not at an elite level, but I was competitive.

"Good," he said, "so was I. I was a second team all-American basketball player in college.

"So, I made a game out of selling. I set a point objective for myself everyday. Sometimes 15, sometimes 20, it depends. But, it is always a reach.

"And, I score myself:

• one point for making a phone call

• two points for making a connection

• three points for setting up an appointment

• four points for having the meeting

• five points for making a sale

"So, if I have a goal of 15 points and am just starting, I have to make sure I have a list of 15 people to call. As I get further in the process, I obviously get more points for connections, appointments, and meetings. So, I have a choice of increasing my goal, or taking a little time to play golf, or to see a friend for lunch.

"In any case, I never, never leave work until I've reached that day's goal."

No wonder he is number one in the world. A version of this might help you achieve the network numbers you need.

How many do you need? We don't know. How long is a piece of string?

We do know that we have clients who have had over 150 informational interviews, let alone follow-ups. And, we do know that job searches take two to four months for the majority, and over six months for some. It partly depends on luck, but it certainly is affected by persistence and stamina. You should recognize, up front, that your job search may take a long time. We recommend sticking to the search for *The Right Mountain* as long as you are emotionally and fiscally able, rather than just taking a job, any job.

So you network, you set up informational interviews, you write thank-you notes, and then you do it all over again.

Set up a filing system or three-ring binder to keep all of this straight. In it you'll have a section for each interviewed individual with all relevant data on him or her, the organization (please get background information before the first interview), the meeting, thank-you notes, and follow-ups.

Yes, the follow-up. Keep in touch to let people who have helped you know how you are doing.

"Just a note to say thank you. You suggested I contact Kay McGill at The Real Estate Company. We had a great meeting and we plan to meet again."

Again, this is not just common courtesy, but it may stimulate something in the recipient's mind.

An important thing to remember is that small organizations, especially those with less than 50 people (the primary hirers these days), create most of the jobs today. Few of these organizations have human resources departments or personnel staff. Few have finite organization charts. All have needs and, because they have to remain flexible to compete, all are looking for a competitive advantage. Usually, this comes in the form of people, not products.

So, if you go for an informational interview, and you know who you are and can articulate it effectively, it will often reveal a need in the organization. The interviewer can then turn the meeting into a job interview!

As an aside, I mentioned earlier that I discovered that I was a Wagon Master while I was volunteering. Peter, one of our clients, volunteered at his local elementary school to help kids with math. He did such a good job, and liked it so much, that he was hired as a tutor, and then given a job offer. Volunteering not only helps you meet new people, but it also helps reaffirm your skills, builds your confidence, and gives you accomplishments. It is something you might consider.

Let me give you another example of how you can create a job.

Michael finished our program and knew he wanted to transfer from sales to being a teacher. Not just any kind of teacher, but one in a school that had a strong outdoor program (his interest area) and believed in experiential education.

After much informational interviewing, he was pointed towards Lakefield College. He was also given an introduction to the principal. He phoned three times and finally made contact. He asked for an informational interview. The principal said there were no openings, budget was restricted, it was a residential school and there were no extra beds, etc, etc. Michael repeated he only wanted an informational, not a job interview. The principal finally relented, primarily as a favor to the individual who referred Michael. But he said it would be a waste of a two-hour drive, still trying to say no. Michael said no problem. He'd love a drive in the fall.

Michael arrived early and had a chance to listen to some of the kids talking about their outdoor programs, the good and the bad. He noted areas where he could add value.

The interview started badly when the principal was late and said he had a crisis, so he only had 15 minutes. He was sorry.

Michael adjusted his planned agenda.

Quickly he asked why the school was so committed to experiential education and what were the gaps. Here he referred to the information the kids had given him. Before long they were in an animated discussion about the plans the principal had for the winter, the spring, and next year! And the fact that he was short of experienced staff.

Michael responded enthusiastically with other program concepts (from his accomplishments) and offered to write curriculum notes. Forty-five minutes later they were touring the school facilities, looking for physical elements that were already on site that could be incorporated into the new programs—the small river that ran through the campus, the ponds that were off limits (we could have a community service project to clean it up!), and on and on.

Eventually they discovered a storage room with a window in the attic of one building, a small room that, with a little paint, could be a cramped bedroom—no problem for Michael.

Money was still an issue, but Michael countered that it might be months before he got another offer, so he would work for room and board!

A deal was struck. Michael moved in the next week.

The informational interview led to a discussion of ideas, which led to Michael's accomplishments, which led to an unknown need, which led to solutions for the sleeping and food problems.

Michael did a great job and within a month the principal found the money to pay him.

The right person, the right place, the right experience, the right attitude. Turning an informational interview, at the interviewer's discretion, into a job interview.

We have dozens of stories like this. It works.

But what about the job interview, the pure job interview?

Read on.

CHAPTER FIFTEEN

The Job Interview
and the Offer

Everything, absolutely everything, is directed at getting the job interview. And now that you have one, you have to turn it into a job offer.

How? Well, let's look at how this might happen.

First, the interview.

Purpose

- You are there to create interest in you, your skills, and your relevant accomplishments.

- You are there to uncover as much information as possible about the company, job openings, and required skills.

- You want the outcome of this "business discussion" to be the conclusion that they need you and want you.

Thus, you are not asking for a job. Rather, you are talking to them and they are deciding to offer you a job.

Preparation

Everything that you have done in this book is in preparation for the interview. Be sure you:

- Can confidently deliver your capsule profile, either in Reference Point or allegorical form.

- Know the company, its needs, and its culture, so you can relate your accomplishments to them.

- Know all you can about the interviewer or interviewers.

- Know all you can about the market, the competition, and the industry's prospects.

The Interview

Because this is a job interview, not an informational interview, the agenda will be set by the interviewer.

The key, from your perspective, is that the interviewer knows:

- Who you are

- What you have accomplished

- How your accomplishments are relevant to their needs

Our conversations after job interviews consistently reveal that:

- The interviewers remember only one or two things about the prospect.

- The interviewees always wish they had remembered to talk about at least one other accomplishment.

So, be the exception. Make sure they remember your most salient selling points: your capsule profile and relevant accomplishments. Prioritize what you want to talk about, so you don't forget anything important.

There should be no rambling, no verbiage, that is not directly relevant to the subject, at least on your part.

You must be enthusiastic, interested, sincere, and succinct. That's why we spend so much time getting you comfortable with the words you are going to use. As a result, you won't find yourself. after the meeting saying, "Why didn't I say this and that?" But you must also be comfortable, humble, and confident.

Is there a typical structure for a job interview? Yes, but, there are always exceptions. Be adaptable and flexible.

Normally, an interview will last 30–45 minutes.

• Three to four minutes of small talk, during which an initial assessment is being made, especially by the interviewer. Be relaxed, focused, and prepared. Ask about personal things in his office to show you are observant and that you care.

• Two minutes, at the most, to recap why you are there.

• Three minutes of your introduction of yourself—your capsule profile. This may come here, if asked for, or it may come after you ask questions and the interviewer show interest.

• You ask questions about the interviewer, the company, and, if there is a job opening, about the job.

• Back and forth questions about yourself, your accomplishments, and their relevance.

- If it seems to be dragging on, cut it off. By doing this, you reveal your sensitivity to the value of the interviewer's time, and, you give him or her the option to start it up again.

Remember, the employer is looking for:

Initiative	Leadership	Judgment
Problem Solving	Decision-Making	Enthusiasm
Communication Skills	Adaptability/Versatility	

These are demonstrated not only by your experience, but also by the interview itself:

- Are you poised, articulate, friendly?

- Do you ask questions that reflect preparation and have a logical progression?

- Do you appear quietly confident?

- Do you demonstrate enthusiasm and sincere interest?

- Do you listen and respond?

- Do you have pride in your accomplishments?

- Do you understand the employer's needs and have the desire to serve them?

- Do you have a good attitude and sound ideas?

- Are you credible?

- Do you take control when appropriate?

In addition, the interviewer is noting:

- Body language—nervous movements—twisting hair; rolling rings; flicking specks off clothes; drumming fingers; looking away; laughter at odd occasions

- Interpersonal skills—monopolizing conversation; interrupting the interviewer

- Style—inappropriate clothing (too formal, too casual); canned rather than conversational answers

You may be asked to fill out an application form depending upon the job you are talking about. If it includes questions on skills and accomplishments, ask if you could take it away to complete. We suggest you type or at least print the form. Use the answers from your résumé as a base for everything you do.

Potential Potholes

Over the years, our conversations with interviewers have revealed an amazing consistency in the failures of the interviewees. Some of the potential potholes include:

- The inability to say "I did it" or "how well I did it." This is, perhaps, the one time in your life when you are allowed to, even have to, brag about what you have done. And it is difficult because we've spent our lives being told not to boast.

- The explanation of why you don't have a job yet or why you left your last job. Be honest: "I haven't found what I want yet, and I want it to be the right job"

- Poor appearance

- Being late for the interview

- Overbearing, too aggressive (attitude/demeanour), ill mannered

- Poor treatment of the receptionist or secretary (who are often asked for their comments)

- Failure to look the interviewer in the eye

- Limp handshake

- Sloppy résumé or application form

- Lack of enthusiasm

- No direction to interview; interviewer has to carry it

- Negative comments about other interviews and/or people

- Overemphasis on money

- Arguing with the interviewer

- Rambling conversation

Questions to Expect

Preparation is key to any meeting, any interview. Our research shows that you might expect any or all of the following questions, some of which are useful, some of which are time fillers. Use the opportunity of answering a question to sell yourself. When I used to train politicians in interviewing skills, I always encouraged them to answer any non-specific questions with a sales pitch for the issue, in this case your accomplishments, they were trying to put forward.

- What career goals have you established?

- What accomplishments do you have that are relevant to us?

- What do you know about us?

- Why are you approaching us?

- What mistakes have you made? What have you learned from them?

- How would your friends describe you?

- Where else would you work if we don't employ you?

- What questions do you have for me?

- Do you work well under pressure?

- In what ways will your education help you on the job?

- What other kinds of jobs are you considering?

- What did you dislike most about your previous job?

- In retrospect, would you do things differently in your last job? How?

- How do you react in a job you don't like?

- What is the best way to hire people?

- What is most important in hiring people?

- How would you fire someone?

- What kind of leader are you?

- What do you do in your leisure time?

- What is your strongest qualification for this job?

The answers you give should include positive, relevant examples of your accomplishments to prove/reinforce/back up your response. They should be from your history and should be specific. Preparation is the key here. You should not be caught by surprise on any question.

While the answers are important, so are other elements of the interview:

- First impressions: appearance; bearing; manners; opening remarks

- Smooth presentation: low stress on both sides

Is It the Right Offer?

Now you have the offer. Your first inclination is to grab it and get to work.

But whoa!

If you are a recent graduate and just want to get started, you might decide to just take the job and get going. We won't argue too strongly on this, but we'd still push you to ensure that you match up your skills, interests, values, and relationships with the job and the organization. It's a real downer to hate your first job, or to get fired because it is a bad fit.

While in high school, Suzi found that she loved advertising. She didn't know if it could be a career, or if she would always enjoy it, but it was a start.

She got an Arts degree in university, but just in case, updated her word-processing and bookkeeping skills.

Upon graduation, she blitzed every ad agency in her city. In each case, she asked for a trainee's job, but added that she had secretarial skills.

No job.

After three months and several return visits, she got an offer for a job as a receptionist. She started on Monday.

She loved it: the people, the action, everything. She enrolled in a broadcast production course on Tuesday nights and a copywriting course every other Thursday.

A year later, her creative interests had been noticed (she kept asking questions of agency people about her courses), her willingness to do extra work had been appreciated, and she asked for an interview with the creative director.

He said he'd keep his eyes open for her, and six months later she was offered a junior copywriting position.

If it is not your first job and you really want to make a better job and career decision, you now have the tools to do so.

When you have a job offer, lay your Reference Point and/or Personal Allegory down on top of it. Does it match? Is it a good fit on the core elements of you: your Core Skills, Core Interest areas, and Core Values. Does there seem to be a match with the people relationship part of it?

This is crucial. Your Reference Point and your allegory helped you get a job offer, now you have to decide if it is the right job for you. Let me again use my personal experience to illustrate how this can be done.

After I had found the Wagon Master template, and before I started The Career Centre, I was winding up some consulting projects that I had done for a venture capital company on the west coast.

One of the clients I had worked with was a software developer in Chicago. They had created the first automatic telephone dialing program that had the ability to recognize the difference between busy signals, answering machines, and a live person. This meant that the computer would know not to make a connection, thus saving time and increasing the efficiency of their operators.

Major banks loved the efficiency of this program in chasing delinquent or overdue credit card bills and the business was booming.

The entrepreneurs who had created the programs knew they couldn't manage a growing business. I had done some consulting with them, they knew I had run a big advertising agency, and, in typical entrepreneurial fashion, they offered me the job of running the company without doing a real job description or search.

I laid the Wagon Master template down on top of the job, assessed the matches in skills, interests, and values, and said no.

They were flabbergasted, and dismayed. I was a known entity to them and the transition would be easy. They offered more money, more stock. I tried to tell them that I wasn't the right person for the job.

"Look," I said, "thank you very much, I'd love to work with you and it is a great business. But I'm the wrong guy.

"You love the Wagon Master allegory, but you don't need a Wagon Master. Your business is growing so fast you need, in allegorical terms, the equivalent of the mayor of a small town in the wild west.

"You need someone to start setting up the infrastructure, bring in the railroad, hire a sheriff, do a town plan. Wagon Masters don't do infrastructure.

"I can help the business grow, get more people on the wagon train, but without the infrastructure, the systems, the controls, the business plans, the checks and balances, you will implode.

"You don't need me, you need a mayor."

They were sad, even upset. And they disagreed with me.

They hired a guy out of Time-Life, a guy much like me, and within a year the business had grown incredibly but, with no infrastructure, it imploded. The pieces were bought up by a vulture fund.

Is the job you are looking at the right job, the right career, the right organization? *The Right Mountain?* Is it a good match?

Go back to what you have done right, your Reference Point or your Personal Allegory, and see if there is a match.

If it fits, great. Take the job!

If it doesn't fit, think long and hard. You probably won't like the job if it doesn't match your skills, interests, and values, and if you don't like it, you won't do well.

And if you don't do well you will quit or get fired.

And start the cycle all over again.

CHAPTER SIXTEEN

Balance and Life Decisions

W̲hat is this thing called Balance? Well, to us, the definition is: being happy, satisfied with where you are and what you are doing.

A lack of balance occurs when you are doing something and think you should be doing something else. You are at the office and you think you should be at your daughter's soccer game. You are out for dinner and you think you should be at home helping with your son's science project. You have just returned from a friend's country place and you think you should be able to afford one too. You are at home cutting the grass and you think you should be at the office preparing for tomorrow's presentation.

And you worry, you fret, get anxious about whether you are doing the right thing or not.

Many seem to think balance is a 50/50 split of time and/or energy between home and work. It is not. Balance is an agreement you, and those that are important to you, reach on priorities. And these priorities change as circumstances change.

My friend Pat says there are four legs on her Balance stool:

Her family

Her job

Her friends

Her personal time

And when she gets out of balance, her weight balloons.

Balance is hardly ever, if there are four legs on your stool, 25%, 25%, 25%, and 25%. It is a moving ratio.

When Pat became CEO and moved to a new city, her priorities were her job and her family; friends and personal time had to take a back seat. She had to acknowledge this, talk to her friends and hope they would understand, or she would be worrying about them when she was supposed to be doing her job. She would be anxious, not in Balance.

When my youngest daughter, Boo, was stricken with the bone-eating disease, and was in hospital for five weeks, I, and all our family, were under huge stress. I tried to keep working, visit her, and keep in touch with my friends. I couldn't do it all, so I was out of balance. I had to rethink my priorities, change the percentage of time allocated to each of the legs of the stool. I talked to my clients and took a leave of absence from work. I talked to my friends and told them that I was basically going to move into the hospital for as long as it took.

The family pulled together. Obviously there was stress and anxiety but I was able to stay in the hospital and focus on her, never once thinking I should be somewhere else. My balance was 90% Boo, with a little bit for myself and the rest of the family, for about five weeks. Eventually we got the disease under control and we were all able to go back to a more normal life. If I had not been able to sort through these priorities, and be comfortable with them, I would not have been able to find balance in these very stressful times.

It is fair to say both Pat and my situations were extreme cases and therefore priorities were probably easier to establish. I agree, but it is amazing how many times people regret their actions, even in extreme cases.

But what about the run of the mill, everyday decisions? What about the basic life decisions? What about Balance then?

Well, this is where all the work you have done to this point comes into play. This is the time to use *Where have I gone right?* as your template. Your Reference Point and your Personal Allegory vividly and simply illustrate your Core Skills, Core Interests and Core Values. And these will help you make decisions without regret, reducing stress and anxiety.

These will help you have the *life you want.*

Let me use some of my own decisions to demonstrate.

On the assumption that you now know me quite well, as the "teaching Bobby how to swim guy" or "the Wagon Master," let's use these templates to test some life issues. Here are some decisions I have had to make:

United Way

When I owned my advertising agency, I was asked to sit on the United Way board, with 48 other people. It sounded good at first, because it was a well-respected not-for-profit that presumably helped people.

But I soon ran into trouble:

- Forty-eight board members—so much for control of my own destiny.

- The *process* was the key agenda focus, not the *people.*

- It not only didn't need, it didn't want, my persuading, inspiring skills. It wanted administration skills, not my long suit.

Home Address

When we decided to move to the country, the location was the first issue. If prestige and status had been my or my wife's Core Values, we would have bought a small property in one of the wealthy enclaves around Toronto. We didn't. We bought a old farm house in a rural area with an address not known by many. And we loved it.

Vacation Home

I bought my brothers out of the old family cottage north of Toronto. It is on a lake where the maximum boat horsepower allowed is 20, so there are no big fancy boats. There are no big-name golf courses. The cottages are small, rustic I guess, rather than big log-and-stone monster homes. Again, a fit with my, and our, values.

This probably points out most dramatically the need to have matching values between spouses or partners.

Office Address

I've owned my own businesses for over 36 years and they have always been in the mid-range rent districts, not the prestige addresses. This is consistent with my values and proves that prestige or status are not important to me.

Volunteer Activities

Over the past several years, I have wanted to get involved in the volunteer community again. Unfortunately all the opportunities seemed conflicted with my Core Values of control of my destiny and making a real difference. Either they were bureaucratic organizations with red tape and hierarchies, or they controlled my access to the final recipients—the people. So I didn't feel I could make a real difference. I kept looking. Finally I found the opportunity.

I met a guy named Peter Dalglish one day, and we hit it off. We decided to create a program to help kids from the inner city become contributing members of their communities. Together with my son Jimmy, we created Trails Youth Initiatives. Soon after we started, Peter left to go on to new adventures.

Today, Trails is a highly acclaimed program.

Was it a good fit for me? You bet. As founding chairman, I operated independently and the program has made a real difference in the lives of some kids, two of my Core Values.

Being small, it was all about the people, not policies, procedures, and bureaucracy, so it fit my interest area.

And it required all my skills to help develop curriculum, hire staff, convince parents to enroll their kids in a new, untested program, and, perhaps most importantly, to raise the $5 million we have needed over the last dozen years.

Interestingly, and perhaps not surprisingly, Trails is based on *The Right Mountain* principles, helping individuals understand who they are and what they can do.

Again and again I have taken "the Wagon Master" and/or "teaching Bobby how to swim" templates and matched them up with challenges, opportunities, and decisions. They have always helped me make good choices, without regret and with great satisfaction.

Try it yourself. It works.

PART

THREE

WHERE HAVE I
GONE RIGHT?

CHAPTER SEVENTEEN

Conclusion

*T*he *Right Mountain* book illustrated that life, in total and in segments, is a journey, not a destination.

Obviously, *Where Have I Gone Right?* is also a journey, not a finite process. You have started the journey, and, while it will lead to jobs and perhaps life decisions, it is, in fact, still a journey.

You started out by looking at where you had gone right, your Core Accomplishments, the times of genuine satisfaction in your life. And you then teased these apart to find your Core Skills, Core Interest areas, and Core Values. You have found the characteristics of your best relationships. And you have found how to describe yourself to others, and to yourself, in ways that are unique.

You now have, as one of our clients described it, handrails to help life decisions. And this is obviously important whether you are 22 or 62.

If you are looking for a job, then this has offered a disciplined approach to job search that, when followed, gives you both the methodology and the confidence to seek that more satisfying job, career, and organization. If you are making life decisions, searching for balance, you now have the tools to make the best, the most satisfying choices.

And when you are satisfied, you will be motivated. And when you are motivated, you will be successful.

There will always be decisions to make, that's why this is a journey. And now you have the tools to make them, on your terms.

On your terms, and surely that is the most important measurement. We believe that

True Success is

the attainment of purpose

without compromising

Core Values

If this definition helps you, then please use it on your journey to *The Right Mountain*.

One of the great joys of The Career Centre is to have graduates come back to talk to current clients, to challenge them and to provide them with support.

Maybe we can start an e-mail network support system for those using this book. Just contact me at jim@therightmountain.com if you would like to be a part of this group.

So, that's it. *Where Have I Gone Right?* is, for most, a different way of figuring out how to make better career and life decisions.

I have long been accused of looking at the glass as neither half full nor half empty, but rather as always filling up. That's because I always look at the good things, the *right* things.

As we have noted earlier in this book, when we come to difficult crossroads in life, particularly when it is precipitated by an unexpected and unhappy event, it becomes human nature to say, "Where have I gone wrong?" or "what did I do to deserve this?"

These are not only the wrong questions to ask, but they are 180° in the wrong direction and they lead up a dead-end street.

You won't find positives by looking at negatives.

Look for the *right* things in your life, and build on them.

And it is a heck of a lot more fun looking at the good times, the right times.

Where have I gone right?

We think it's a better way to look at life.

Index

CONTACT US

Over the past decade and a half, I have had the privilege of helping hundreds of people through life, career and job transitions. Each of them came to The Career Centre on the recommendation of someone else—a friend who had been through the program, someone I knew from my past business life, someone who had heard or read *The Right Mountain*....

I wrote this book for those who couldn't come and meet me in person, who couldn't sit in my office and tell me their story. These people were looking for more than just someone who would say, "You should do this…This is your next job…Your life will be this." Sure, they wanted to know *what* they were going to do. But they also wanted to know *why*. And that's why I almost always started the conversation with—you guessed it—*Who are you?*

Those who have met me or heard me speak, know that this book is written in my own voice. It's how I talk. And so it's a conversation between you and me, just as it would be in my office.

But we would love to hear your voice, too! And we at *The Right Mountain* are creating ways for your learning—and ours—to extend beyond this book. We do that through seminars and workshops; our Web site and its developing online communities; through our speeches and presentations; through our audio and video materials; posters; workbooks and more.

So please go to our Web site, or contact our office for more information on how to take *Where Have I Gone Right?*—and your life—to the next level.

And please keep in touch to let me know personally how you are doing. I can be reached directly at jim@therightmountain.com or the number and address below.

The Right Mountain
378 Fairlawn Avenue • Toronto, Ontario • M5M 1T8
Tel: 416-785-7700 • Fax: 416-785-3854
www.therightmountain.com